# A Good Death:
# A Memoir on the Life of An Avatar
## (Helen P. Kipp, 1932-1995)

Book One of
The Avatar Chronicles

By
**Frederick R. Kipp**

ISBN: 0-75965-801-3

This book is printed on acid free paper.

1stBooks - rev. 08/31/01

For Jeffery

# CONTENTS

## PART FIVE: THE WORK

## PART SIX: SYNTHESIS

"An Avatar is a Being Who-having first developed His Own nature, human and divine, and then transcended it- is capable of reflecting some cosmic Principle or divine quality and energy which will produce the desired effect upon humanity, evoking a reaction, producing a needed stimulation and, as it is esoterically called, 'leading to the rending of a veil and the permeation of light.'"

Alice A. Bailey
*The Externalisation of the Hierarchy*

# INTRODUCTION

"Venus, Virgo, Mercury, Mars!   Venus, Virgo, Mercury, Mars!"   As I entered her room, I heard Helen yell these words repeatedly.   From the hoarseness of her voice and the tension of the others in the room, I could tell that this seemingly incoherent repetition had been going on for some time.   Ann approached me and told me that Helen had started speaking these words softly, well over an hour ago.   Gradually she became louder and more agitated.   Nothing she did helped to calm Helen.   Ann's nerves were raw and she was on the verge of tears.   For several months I had stayed close to Helen because somehow my presence seemed to comfort her.   However, today was her birthday and I took a few hours out to shop for a birthday gift.

As Ann left the room, I placed a chair close to Helen's bed, sat down and took her hand.   She had never been so agitated.   It seemed as if she was in a trance and nothing I said registered with her.   Day by day, the person I knew as Helen had drifted farther and farther away from her body and from me.   For the past few months I had done everything I could think of to stimulate her to return, and today it seemed as if she had left for good.   While praying for guidance and her relief, suddenly my confusion cleared and I understood what was happening.

Helen was using this simple astrological mantra to connect with and anchor her consciousness in her physical body sufficiently to speak with me.   I told her this and immediately her agitation dissipated.   She continued to speak the same series of words over and over for another fifteen to twenty minutes, but now in a rather calm and determined way.   Then in a soft, tentative but distinct voice of the person I knew as Helen she said, "Fred, I am tired and I am going to die." Finally she asked me to let her go so she could die, then went on to tell me how this would happen.   I was stunned and devastated!

It was her sixty-third birthday and the only gift she wanted from me was to let her die.   This was the saddest and most painful day of my life.   With our marriage, I accepted a sacred trust for her care and keeping from God.   To the best of my ability, for over seventeen years I kept this trust as her husband, her student and in service to her work.

Helen died on the morning of February 19, 1995.   Death came in the way she had described and as quickly as the doctors had predicted.   Why would anyone have thought otherwise?   Although life threatening, her known ailments were treatable.   However, she had refused medical treatment and anyone who saw her could see the signs of death in her body.   I also saw those signs, but I did not see death.   I saw only the life and Spirit of a remarkable person who gave the Christ freedom to transform her physical body according to her covenant with God.

ix

Many people make promises to God, but few live them and back them up with their physical life. She did!

In this memoir I attempt to explain Helen's covenant with God and why she was willing to die to fulfill it. I tell her story primarily from my experiences with her and from our in-depth conversations about her life and experiences over the years. My recollections are augmented by her journals and her other written materials I inherited upon her death. My intent is to present insights into her life and psyche through events she identified as pivotal in her growing awareness of God through the spiritual forces guiding her life and work.

Helen's initial commission from God was to help others see the beauty and transforming power of their internal God Self. As a spiritual teacher, she helped people learn how to give this Higher Self the freedom to transform their lives. Her method was to teach through living the principles of personality transformation and by surrendering ever deeper to the Christ. She did this openly and in plain sight of her students and others in her life. Her way was one of actively doing and then talking about it from her own practical experience.

Helen did not see herself as being a special human being and had great difficulty acknowledging and accepting the higher levels of consciousness expressing through her. In fact, she believed that if she could do anything for God, then certainly others could also. Helen claimed no divinely inspired power and authority for anyone other than herself. She valued anonymity and truly loved doing much of her job silently and privately. On the Initiatory Path of Life, Helen was led beyond personality change into dense physical transformation. This became her individual work and life focus. Through God, she cooperated with the Christ energy working through the Holy Spirit to raise and refine the matter of her physical body. Helen referred to this process as building a "New Body" pattern that would also be used to create the physical bodies for future evolutionary races of human beings.

This book does not contain much detail about the New Body work nor does it explain the full extent of what we learned in the process. That is better left to another book at another time. However, some context in Helen's New Body work is necessary to tell the story. Therefore, I try to explain briefly some far-reaching metaphysical concepts and perspectives. For those interested in this aspect of her life, you will not find these explanations sufficient. I have included some further reading suggestions at the end of the book.

Since I am part of Helen's story, I am not an objective observer. So please keep this in mind as I relate details of Helen's life. Although she and I discussed most aspects of her life, the things that stood out to me were those experiences or events that shaped or changed her life in significant ways. Certainly, if you were to speak with others who knew her, their version of the same events and interactions would differ. In my opinion, presenting Helen's perspective of her life experiences is essential in understanding how they contributed to the person known as Helen. Although I was a part of her life, this memoir is about Helen. Therefore, I have chosen to write about myself as any other person in her life.

Since inner energy life is real for me, I do not consider it mysterious, exalted or superior. Because of this, I often write about inner life realities in a matter-of-fact way. However, by no means do I have all the answers. Daily, I go through my own process of interpretation, analysis, internalization and synthesis of my experiences for deeper meaning and answers. This always leads me to new questions. The result is that I continue to live my life in a state of constant change. My only certainty is that there is a God and that Its energy will reveal to me only what I need to know and do in my own life.

Lastly, but perhaps most importantly, the personal and inner spiritual experiences in this book represent our life reality only. I do not expect anyone to accept them as fact or truth for themselves. If they are of any value to anyone, it is because that person found some internal resonance within the underlying energy and checked it out through their own spiritual guidance. Some people may find parts of this book unbelievable or even incredible science fiction. I can certainly understand that response. Helen's life was indeed radical. All I can say is that I've tried to tell her life story as she shared it, and the work as we lived it. Now, on with the story.

# PART ONE:

# INTO THIS WORLD

*Frederick R. Kipp*

# Chapter One

"These people don't like me!" That was Helen's first impression of her new life and her first contact with her parents. She felt as if immediately neither her mother nor her father wanted her or knew what to do with her. For Helen, the strength of this experience set the underlying tone of difficulty between them. Of course, as the baby Helen, she was unable to experience much other than her new and yet unfinished little body. However, as the inner being Helen connected to that body, somehow she was able to use its physical presence in the external world to perceive and experience people, events and her environment.

An infant's silent awareness of its inner being usually fades as its body gains physical strength and independence through cultural conditioning by family and society. In Helen's case, though, she never completely lost contact with that inner dimension of her being. Therefore, she could remember many significant early physical experiences as well as some of her inner life as a spiritual being apart from her physical, human identity. This connection with her Spiritual Self remained her center throughout her life. As it developed and strengthened, its active presence gave depth to her spiritual purpose and was the source of much of her spontaneity and joy in living. In following its guidance, however, Helen's behavior was often unconventional. This was the source of considerable confusion and misunderstanding in others about who she was and how she lived her life.

As Helen grew into childhood, time and again she confirmed her initial impressions of her parents' reactions and rejection of her. She was always quick to note that farm life in rural Tennessee during the early thirties was difficult at best. The Great Depression made farm life even harder. When Helen was born on January 5, 1932, people were already struggling to make a living, to put food on the table and to keep their spirits up to lessen the suffering and hardship for their children. Helen's parents, Walter and Alene Pirtle, were no different in this respect.

Life in West Tennessee farm country was probably much like life in many rural communities in America at that time. The county seat was the focus of local government, law enforcement and commerce in the county. Scattered throughout the countryside, small Christian churches were the centers of religious worship, social interaction and the moral compass for the community. Most of the smaller farming communities had their own one-room schoolhouse to teach children up to high school. The larger towns in the area were the sites of regional county or city high schools. It was common at the time to see farmers walking behind a team of mules ploughing their fields. The whole family

3

worked on the farm and being a girl did not cut one much slack when it came to farmwork. Everyone worked! During planting and harvest times, the school year was set up with time off so children could help in the fields.

With the responsibilities of a farm and family, her father's burdens were sizable. Helen thought that many of her early problems with him related to his disappointment that she wasn't a boy who in time could help relieve him of some of the burdens in his life. To make matters worse, Helen's sisters Doris and Norma were born into the family in the following years. This meant that all hope of having a son to pass on his love of farming as well as to help him with the farmwork vanished for her father.

Helen was especially sympathetic towards her mother and her difficult role in life. After discussions with her mother, other family members and friends, Helen later realized that her mother was unprepared for her challenging and difficult life as a farm wife and mother. Besides her tasks of cooking, cleaning and childcare, she had to tend to the family's vegetable garden as well as can food for the winter. During very active or difficult crop cycles, she also worked in the fields while supervising the children. She was barely able to cope with the hardships of her life and then she had Helen to care for. Trying to give her mother the benefit of understanding, Helen always felt that perhaps this was at least part of the source of her mother's early rejection of her.

Helen truly loved her parents, probably more deeply than either of them could have imagined. She was an exceptionally sensitive child. From an early age she could see past people's behavior to the beauty of their inner spiritual being. Despite how she was treated by others, she used this inner beauty as an anchor for her love. She also seemed to have a depth of maturity as well as a sense of fairness and judgment far beyond her age. When she experienced injustice in her mother's or father's treatment of her, rather than rebel outwardly she went deep inside and closed herself off to either or both of them. As a result, she became quite internally independent of her parents and learned how to live without approval from others.

Her mother reacted to her withdrawals by trying to break Helen's spirit. As Helen saw it, this behavior injected an element of psychological survival into her life. Her spirit was all she had that was her own and she felt she couldn't go on living if it was taken from her. This created a battle of wills between her and her mother. At one point it was so intense that her mother locked her in a closet for many hours to punish her for something Helen did in the kitchen. Aimed to make Helen more submissive, this kind of punishment never worked, which further infuriated her mother. Probably out of desperation more than anything else, they came to an accommodation - as long as Helen yielded the kitchen as her mother's domain, a level of harmony existed between them.

4

Apparently Helen's innate sensitivities included an ability to tune into other people's silent thoughts and feelings in a way that enabled her to know the essence of their character. Perhaps this early ability to see her parents so clearly was more than she or either of her parents could cope with at the time. Facing this type of psychic power in an adult would have been intimidating enough, but to experience it in their first born, child must have been especially threatening for them. At the age of six Helen realized that the only way to maintain some kind of family peace and happiness was for her to change. Therefore, she learned to yield superficial aspects of herself to her parents and behave in a manner to appease them. She just set her course towards her eventual freedom when she was old enough, and moved forward accordingly in her life.

Even with all the difficulties she and her parents had, Helen loved living on the farm. She always considered her farm life experiences as the source of her sense of practicality, resourcefulness and willingness to work hard for what she valued in life. As with many farm children of the time, the fact of a national economic depression was lost on Helen. Because of the efforts of her mother and father, the family always had enough food to eat and clothes to wear. Their entertainment needs were few and fulfilled by family, school and church activities. Life on the farm was all that she knew and in many ways it was an externally sheltered and happy existence. Because of this, Helen lived in a world of her own.

Although she liked people, she talked more to the little nature forms and spirits in the trees and earth than to anyone else. Somehow, she came into this world without the normal human filters and barriers between the invisible and visible realms of life. Therefore, automatically and with great ease she saw past the external form of nature into the spiritual dimensions behind it. It was in this inner spiritual realm that she spoke to the little beings giving life to the natural beauty all around her. They became her friends and accepted her in a way that she did not find in the human world. If she needed help with something, she received it unquestionably. Her relationship with these nature beings taught her emerging human spirit as well as nurtured and healed her growing physical body. Through this experience, she developed a secure sense of wholeness within herself and a oneness with all life. Many years later she discovered that this was her first experience with the Holy Spirit as it expressed through nature.

Like most children, she was inquisitive and had many questions about these early spiritual experiences and wondered why others didn't speak of them. She believed them normal to all people. When questioned by Helen, her parents dealt with her experiences as fanciful and therefore offered very few thoughtful or meaningful replies. Although the family was very religious, her early church conditioning was confusing since her parents were members of different Protestant churches. Each believed theirs was the true Christian way to salvation and that any other way was damned. In one of her written notes, she states that "this conflict of doctrinal belief put the family in a constant state of religious cold war."

Overwhelmed by the enormous Spirit of God, it was unthinkable to Helen that anyone who believed could not find personal comfort, guidance and salvation within this magnificent Presence. She questioned why it was so important to her parents to have a sense of "being in the right" with God. In Sunday School, she learned that all those who believe in the Christ have everlasting life. Each of her parents believed in Jesus Christ, so something must be very wrong or at the least misinterpreted.

Even though her parents were in disagreement about religion, they agreed in their disapproval of Helen's relationship and communication with nature beings. As a child she could not understand why it was so wrong to see and experience the Spirit of God all around her. It was there and she knew it beyond any doubt, no matter what others believed or said. She had to be true to the way she experienced God's presence in the world. If she was, she believed that someday she would understand these differences in perception.

On her broader and more worldly questions, her mother did not have the time or patience to answer her and her father gave her information that was easily verifiable as wrong. With this kind of response, it did not take long for Helen to learn to keep to herself. When she didn't understand something about the world, she talked to God in her heart about it. As difficult as it was at the time to be rebuffed so thoroughly by her parents, it would later prove to be a gift from God. For the rest of her life she would automatically go into the heart and mind of God to get the answers she needed.

As a child she especially liked to lie down in the freshly plowed fields and feel the power of the earth all around her. At times when she was feeling ill, she would ask the Spirit of the Earth for healing. She said she could feel its healing radiation in and around her body and was healed many times in this way. Another favorite place for her was in her grandfather's apple orchard. Helen liked to go into the orchard in the late afternoon and play under the trees. At sunset, she climbed into a tree and in the peace and serenity of that special place, she went into her heart and talked to God.

In her later spiritual work, she found this internal God relationship the mainstay of her physical and psychological survival. Although her love of nature never changed throughout her life, her relationship to the natural world changed for the worse. This was extremely painful to Helen and because of this shift, she lost her previous sense of protection in nature. However, even this played an important role in her life by making it necessary to discover other creative and healing aspects of God to fill this void.

6

When Helen was about two years old her parents lost their farm, making it necessary for the family to move into a house built by her grandfather next to his farm. Besides farming, her grandfather ran a small country store nearby. When Helen was a little older, she apparently spent much time with him in his store. She found him very disciplined and firm with her but in contrast to her parents, his way was always one of encouragement. Most importantly though was that he did not in any way try to diminish her spirit. Helen wrote about an incident in his store that taught her the value of self-discipline and truly listening to others. She writes:

"I was with him one day in his store and he told me to sit up on the counter so he could polish my badly scuffed shoes. I didn't sit very quietly or very still and once or twice I almost knocked the can of polish off the counter. Finally he said that if I turned over the polish he would stop polishing my shoes. Shortly thereafter I knocked the can off the counter. As he said he would do and without anger or scolding, he simply picked up the can, replaced the lid and left my other shoe unpolished."

His simple and direct response to Helen, taught her that there were consequences to her behavior. From then on, she believed people when they told her something and eventually learned to stop trying to influence or force anyone to change just to get her own way. From this experience she began to learn that when she gave freedom to others, she assured it for herself.

When Helen was about five, the family moved out of their house on her grandfather's farm. This, she was told, was because her father and grandfather could not get along. Even though she didn't understand why they couldn't get along, the fact that they didn't helped her feel less responsible for own problems with her father. Perhaps she wasn't the problem he wanted her to believe. She was unsure how others perceived her father but later it surprised her to learn that many who knew him held him in high regard. In his prime, Helen's father was an imposing man in height and weight. From a purely physical standpoint, people had to look up to him. He lived in a time and area where physical size and strength meant a lot to a man. Perhaps this influenced how others saw him.

Helen suspected that many of her father's early problems with her were because he lacked an education and could not read or write. During his early elementary schooldays, he came down with rheumatic fever which forced him to quit school to stay at home to recuperate. Apparently this took many years and he was not healthy enough to return to school until he was about 12 years old. By this time he had completely missed his elementary education. It embarrassed him to be in class with much younger children and he felt inept and out of place with children of his own age. As a result, his mother took him out of school completely, never to return. This must have made him feel terribly insecure in the community and inferior to his childhood peers. When Helen was older she

7

learned his mother doted on him and made him feel as if everything he did was better than others to help bolster his sense of self esteem.

Perhaps his mother's approach helped him succeed in the world since he grew into a skilled farmer and blacksmith. From outward appearances he may have seemed secure in his manhood and not solicitous of anyone's approval. However, from Helen's description of his "know-it-all" attitude and dictatorial behavior towards her, it did matter to her father how she perceived him. Helen always felt that somehow her insatiable inquisitiveness coupled with his inability to give her answers made him feel inadequate as a man and a father. Apparently his response was to try to squelch her challenging spirit to eliminate its threat to him. From Helen's experience, he did this by building an authoritarian prison around her using his size to intimidate her into submission.

Despite his behavior, Helen wanted to be proud of him, to respect him and to look up to him. His dismissive and overbearing behavior defeated even her most earnest and loving attempts to bond with him. Finally when she was about twelve or thirteen years old, she just stopped trying. By then she had realized that in the areas of moral strength, courage, integrity and the ability to think, sadly she was already a better man then he. This was a very painful and disappointing time for her. She wanted and needed a trusted masculine role model to look to for guidance in her life. Helen could no longer look to her father for this and once again she had to turn within for direction from God.

As an adult her relationship with her father improved even though it was still somewhat strained. This was possible because she was free of his parental authority and he had mellowed with time. Over the years, life taught him many hard lessons he could not have learned any other way. Looking back, Helen said that she learned a very valuable lesson from her father. He introduced her to the masculine attitude and behavior of "might makes right." It was unjust. Somehow inherently she knew that to force someone to your way through physical size or other intimidation was not only pointless but also rendered them captive. For the balance of her life, she stood against this energy in all of its various manifestations in both males and females. She considered this experience with her father the driving force to find and practice true fairness and justice in her relations with all people and events in her life.

# Chapter Two

Helen started school in a one-room school house at Hope Hill, Tennessee when she was five years old. In one of her notes she writes that "I liked this school very much because I was learning to write." In this brief statement Helen reveals a glimpse of what was to become a lifelong love affair with knowledge and learning. This was especially true when what she was learning or experiencing challenged what she believed at the time. Unfortunately, in the middle of that first school year, the family moved to yet another farm about ten miles away and in another county. This change in location meant that she had to change schools. For the time and the area, this was a big transition.

In her new school, children had to be six years old before October to be able to enroll. Rather than making an exception for her since she had already started the school year, officials made her leave school and wait until the following year to begin again. The wait was very difficult on Helen and although her natural curiosity and desire to learn did not change, her attitude about learning did. Perhaps if she been able to remain in school she might have more readily adapted to the teaching methods of the time. As it turned out, the extra year seemed only to enhance her sense of independence.

When she returned to school the following year, her mind had grown past the level of first-year teaching. She learned her lessons but the work did not challenge her growing intuitive mind. Therefore, she easily became bored with her school activities and assignments. Helen said that this was the time in her life when she began to follow the Holy Spirit as her primary teacher in all areas of life. This early orientation and perspective gave her a uniquely different view of her experiences and of all life around her.

Helen overheard a conversation between her parents that made an impact in her life and relationship to God. She writes about it in the following way:

"During the winter around my eighth birthday, I overheard my father and mother talking. A friend of my father told him that in the future people would be able to stand on any spot on the earth and know what everyone who ever stood there had thought. Also, in the future there would be machines built that would do the same thing. Father and Mother thought this was ridiculous but it made an impact on me that changed my life. It caused me to learn how to become conscious of what I thought about anything and everything from that day on. I felt that God knew my every move, thought and feeling and I learned how to live on this basis. This event had more of an effect on my life than anything that I was taught to believe. Looking back I can say from that point on I built my life around a commitment to conscious self-awareness."

In this seemingly ordinary event, Helen was able to find a connection to something deep inside that spoke to her in a way that made a lasting impression on her life. Her response to this experience and other similar events in her life forced her to find her own internal compass - one based on her deep connection with God. While still a young child she began to take responsibility for herself, her thoughts and feelings in a way that contributed to her growing independence and self-reliance.

As Helen grew older she began to experience people and events in ways that cut across the norms of her upbringing. It was as if various unconscious parts of others spoke to her separately from their actual conscious words. These experiences directly exposed and introduced Helen to the confusing and dark realms of the personal subconscious and collective human unconsciousness. She writes about this aspect of her childhood as follows:

"As a child, I always lived in a state of constant confusion. I went through considerable agony over trying to understand and know what other people wanted from me or what they wanted me to do. When someone spoke to me, I heard what they said to me, but their hearts and a different part of them said something else. It was hard for me to sit and listen to someone talk to me smiling while inside they disliked or hated me. This seemed two-faced and it incited hate in me also. It was hard for me to accept and understand that they didn't know they did this. In time, I learned to cope with this situation and to handle my own hurt and hateful feelings as a result. At night when I went to bed, I stood before whoever it was in my mind's eye and from my heart I sent love to them until I didn't hate them anymore."

Somehow, quite automatically, Helen looked for internal ways to change herself and her own feelings about others rather than trying to get others to change their feelings towards her. Although Helen felt the same pain, anguish, and rejection as everyone else, apparently she seemed to know inherently that if she held these reactive emotions within herself, they would destroy her. In another nightly ritual she learned to identify the unreality of those harmful emotions and release them, to be replaced by God's Love. She decided she would rather feel God's Love than hate. If that were true for her, then it must be true for others, and she extended this love to others all her life.

Helen's faith in God to transform or transmute existing negativity into its potential good was enormous. However, it was an intelligent faith. Although she extended love to others, it was not her nature to force others to receive it. It was given unconditionally in the spirit of freedom. Later in her life, though, she discovered that strong personal love could just as easily bind her to others as hate. This love-hate dilemma was resolved for Helen by the Holy Spirit when It

10

taught her to allow the freedom of Christ Love to flow through her rather than personal love. This kind of love is free of restriction to all who use and receive it.

Through the taunting of her schoolmates, Helen soon realized that besides knowing how to love she also needed to learn how to defend herself. She did this in ways that were not always visible or obvious. It was her way to deal with this silently within herself through prayer. Helen believed that with everything that happened to her, she somehow had her own part in it. If there was something in her that needed adjustment, she trusted the Holy Spirit to show her what it was and how to change it. Once revealed, she embraced the need for change and changed with unwavering commitment. She knew that change was in progress when she no longer felt internal disturbance over the incident.

When Helen was about nine years old, she fell in the barn and hit the back of her head on a nail, hard enough to require stitches to close the wound. Falling and requiring minor medical treatment is a common occurrence in childhood. However, after the wound or the scrape heals, all is forgotten and life goes back to normal. The reason this event stood out in Helen's mind as significant was that after the physical wound healed nothing went back to normal. The blow to her head opened up a new and deeper level of her emerging, intuitive life to new dimensions. Through various other accidents and ailments she had visions and experiences with magnificent inner Beings of Light. These episodes strengthened her spirit and gave her much needed encouragement to remain open to her inner life.

Although Helen did not know why, as a child she believed nothing happened, to her or anyone else, by chance or coincidence. With the God she knew, everything had purpose and the Holy Spirit always revealed that purpose to her. Each new inner experience compelled her to reconcile the seen and unseen aspects of life all around her. Being nine years old, the magnitude of this task overwhelmed her. She eventually realized that for her own peace of mind she had to learn to be patient until she was old enough for the Holy Spirit to give her guidance on this matter. Helen's deep desire to learn and grow opened up and set in motion a lifelong path of spiritual education. In the meantime, though, she worked toward trusting the reality of her inner experiences since this was something she never wanted to let others take from her.

To make life easier, Helen hid the reality of her internal life from her family and friends. She adopted an external personality that was friendly, but independent of other people. Because she was not able to talk openly about her sensitivity to the unconscious realms of human life, she kept to herself and had few friends. It wasn't that she did not like people or didn't want to have friends, but rather that her life was much more complex than others her own age. Although a happy child, she approached life more seriously than other children and she easily grew tired of their areas and levels of interest. She found much more internal enjoyment and satisfaction in just thinking about God and the world.

During the solitude of her adolescent life, one of her favorite pastimes was to think creatively about how she would one day escape the restrictions of her life and of the area. She did this by designing houses in her mind. Inspired by the lack of space in her family home, she thought about what it would be like to live in a large house with room for all. Not only did she design these houses in her mind and feelings, she explored what it would be like to live in them also. This simple imaging or visioning technique helped develop and train her creative and intuitive mind.

# Chapter Three

Helen entered her teenage years very naive to social conditioning and norms. She accepted the world at face value and always wanted to believe others. People confused her by speaking in one way and acting in another, sometimes completely contrary to what they said. When she said something she meant it and she thought others did too. Helen had no social role models to teach her about the subtleties of social interaction. Although her social inexperience was troubling to her, it forced her to make decisions for herself. She did this based on the facts and her intuitive perceptions of any situation as she read them, rather than the accepted social rules.

Socially, this did not make Helen popular. She decided to speak truth as she saw it and to live by her spoken words. When she committed to something, she fulfilled that commitment in exactly the way she declared. Because integrity was important to Helen, she held others to what they said while expecting no less from herself. This approach made life very difficult but she could live no other way and internally be satisfied with herself.

At about thirteen or fourteen years old she had an experience with one of her sisters that changed anyone's ability to use or manipulate her again. As the story goes, when her sister couldn't get her way with Helen, she tried to manipulate her emotionally. This soon escalated to the point that her sister threatened to kill herself if Helen didn't comply. This worked for a while but one day she pulled the stunt with a butcher knife. She told Helen that she was going to the barn to kill herself and it would be Helen's fault. Tired of being intimidated, something inside Helen snapped and she told her sister to go ahead and do it. Of course she didn't, but it broke that pattern of behavior with Helen. From the influence of this experience and others, Helen made a personal commitment to work towards not being open to any kind of threat or intimidation from others.

Later, as an adult, Helen found effective nonverbal ways of dealing with subtle attempts to control, coerce or emotionally blackmail her. When it was obvious to her that someone was attempting this, her spine seemed to straighten suddenly as if a rod of steel had just snapped her upright. Then a deafening silence came over her entire being as she deftly but very softly deflected their indirect threat. There was never any doubt in the other person that they had stepped over a dangerous line with Helen and that their manipulation attempt had failed.

Neither of Helen's parents were equipped to comprehend her developing needs as a young woman and to guide her through her teenage years. Helen always said that she doubted any parent of the time would have been better able to help her. Her unique perspective of the many dimensions of life and God set her apart from any standard of norm for the area and her parent's life experience.

For her father, farming and blacksmithing were the only areas in his life where he felt truly secure. His self-worth and identity were bound up in these roles and blinded him to the greater world around him. He believed that girls were incapable of learning to farm but he had no problem using them as laborers. In addition, he made no allowances for their feminine needs, leaving them feeling less than adequate in their work. His general belief was that females taunted males with their bodies. He believed females should always be covered up and carried this to extremes with his daughters. During the first few years of Helen's high-school basketball play, he forbade her to wear the usual gym shorts and insisted she wear blue jeans instead.

In all ways, her father's behavior told her that he did not consider girls or women very smart and certainly not equal to males or men in anything. As a result, he did not believe Helen when she told him things she learned or experienced in school. This was never more painfully true than when she told him the high school principal kept putting his hand on her upper thigh. He accused her of making it up. His attitude and response caused her to feel that if a man made a sexual advance towards her, then she must have done something to cause it. For Helen, experiences like these eroded any sense of lingering trust or respect for her father until there was none left at all. For whatever reason, she came to believe her father did not love her enough to protect her. These experiences forced her to take further steps towards becoming an independent and self-reliant woman. Helen resolved to continue developing herself in a way that nurtured internal satisfaction, self acceptance and self-respect without looking for it from others.

Although her mother had an education, she was very inexperienced in the world outside her local community life. She seemed more concerned with appearances and concealing their farming lifestyle than anything else. As a result, she insisted her girls wear long-sleeved shirts and hats while working in the field. Helen appreciated that this was also a practical matter to protect them from the sun. But, by the way her mother spoke, it seemed she was most interested in preventing others from knowing that they were farmer's children who labored in the sun. Despite the difficulties between her and her mother, she wanted and needed to feel close to her and tried to find something in common to bring them together. However, in response her mother really didn't try very hard to establish a relationship with her. The only area of their life in which she felt motivated to coach her was at church. However, for Helen this was a bittersweet experience. Rather than share her religious life with Helen, she opted to tell

Helen just how to act in church to conform or blend with the behavior of the others.

Helen spoke of one particular church experience with her mother that made a lasting impression. She had joined her mother's church when she was twelve years old. This was a very emotional time for her and emotions ran high during a revival meeting they were attending. Helen loved the Christ and was accustomed to feeling His presence regularly in her life. One night during the revival, her mother, along with other church members, surrounded Helen to talk. They asked her why she didn't want to be saved and why she didn't go up front to the mourners' bench.

This went on for some time and finally, as Helen stated it, "under duress," she went to the bench with the others called to salvation. Interestingly, she said she was drawn towards this and probably would have gone on her own without the adult pressure. She returned up front each meeting for the next three nights. On the final night, everyone shook hands with those from the bench, but not Helen's. She asked her mother why and was told it was because she didn't behave in the right manner. Her mother told her she was to cry like everyone else, and when the preacher touched her, she was to fall back on the floor.

The meeting was ending and she was beginning to fear that she would be the only one left at the bench. Finally a man, sensitive to her predicament, came forward and told her to cry more and then to stand up and tell the minister she had been saved. She did not want to, but finally in emotional desperation she did as she was instructed, but was in anguish over succumbing to this kind of prescribed behavior. In two weeks, all who were saved were to be baptized in the Tennessee River. She was frantic to find a way out but this was impossible without hurting her mother's feelings. So she went ahead with the baptism and came away from the whole experience feeling very hypocritical.

After the baptism service Helen asked her mother why she must act in certain ways to be accepted as saved by others. Her mother said that was simply the way things were done. This was devastating to Helen. She felt her spirituality so deeply inside that to do something simply because it was expected was not only very offensive, but also revolting to her. This was another important lesson for her in integrity. With this experience, she deepened her desire to learn how to live her life in a way that she could be true to herself and the reality of her own relationship with God - not for the acceptance of others.

Although Helen was generally disappointed in her relationship with her mother, she did learn many things. One in particular proved to be of great benefit to her. Every time she asked her mother a question she could not answer, she told Helen to "pray through it" for an answer. Even though it was obvious to Helen that her mother had no idea of the value of what she told her to do, this simple statement became another sustaining staple of her life. Through prayer, she learned to rely on God to answer all of her questions. Helen's internal connection with God's energy was the last word for her on everything. Regardless of the social or economic cost, she learned to live her life based on it.

For the next few years she thought deeply about religion and the ways of her mother's church. After much consideration she decided to leave that church and join her father's church, which she thought wasn't as emotional. It emphasized study of the Bible and used scriptural quotations in the place of emotional pressure to ensure proper Christian behavior. Through this experience, Helen learned the Bible well. This was especially true of the New Testament and she could quote scripture with the best of the members. However, as with her previous church experience, she felt no closer to either parent or to knowing God and this she dearly wanted!

Helen considered all aspects of life to be a vast field of education. She was intensely curious and open to learning in any form and from anyone. During a ninth-grade English class, her teacher taught that, in the study of literature, one must picture in their mind what they were reading so that the subject came alive within you. From this point on, Helen said her relationship with learning leaped forward and wrote "It was as if the doors of my mind opened wide." She applied this visualization process purposefully in everything she wanted to know. All things became alive to her to the point where, if she was not careful, she felt as if she became psychically connected with everything that she was reading. In studying history, these experiences began to transcend the dimensions of time and space. They were so real that she came away feeling as if she had actually been there at the time when the event took place.

Many years later she discovered that these early imagination or visualization experiences opened her up to the truth and reality of reincarnation. Through these exercises, she experienced the recorded energy of past lifetimes in the present. Studying history and learning beyond what was written in books was part of the process of going through or releasing the recorded energy and events from previous lives. These old energies and essences were actually unconscious parts of her that were impinging on and affecting her present life. She learned that this energy from the past was not consciously available to her until she was able to internalize and integrate its lesson and message into her present life.

As she pursued her studies, these visions continued along with other paranormal experiences. While she was contemplating various subjects, she often found herself going into a dream-like dimension where her ability to learn was enhanced greatly. Then at night she began to be aware of separating from her physical body as she went to sleep and awakened each morning remembering her inner world experiences as dreams. Although excited about discovering these new and enriching dimensions, it further complicated her life.

One perplexing problem for her was that what she learned in school about stars and the dimensions of the universe and all life did not reflect what she learned in church and the Bible about God and creation. Somehow, though, she felt them connected anyway. To try to reconcile this, at night she looked up at the stars and asked God in her mind to take her up into the vastness of space and teach her. As God responded and lifted her in consciousness into space, she said that although she had the physical sense of going out to meet the universe, it also seemed as if the universe was within her. While this was happening, she thought about our planet earth going around the sun and then the sun going around something larger taking along its planets with their orbs. In her mind she then explored other dimensions by rearranging things or changing the direction of planetary rotation. She did this until all motion stopped. From that still and silent place, the universe opened up to her to teach her more about God and life.

With Helen's intuitive nature, she preferred to experience life through her mind. The physical activities that others automatically performed took an intense focus of will, discipline and concentration for Helen. Her relationship with her physical body was truly unique. For some reason she never really related to her physical form as being her. It was as if she was always aware that she was only expressing through her body but that it was not her. Although she moved and expressed gracefully, she was not always comfortable in her body and could not automatically get it to move or express as she wanted. As she looked back on her life from her later spiritual perspective, she recognized that this was because she did not connect well to the dense external world through her body. Often it looked to others as if she was slow to learn and clumsy while she was actually intently working on consciously internalizing the principles of some sport or activity. Then all of a sudden, just when others gave up on her, she astounded them with her ability to perform.

A case in point was in high-school basketball. She said she was terrible in practice. Her coach often accused her of being lazy and not concentrating on her playing skills. This was especially so in practice when she missed baskets and generally messed up plays. However, when games came along, she was a standout player and won many games for the team. The problem was that she did not learn from rote practice or develop physical conditioning from repetitive exercise. Somehow, even as a teenager, she had the unique ability to perfect her playing skills and condition her body using mind power. Through her creative mental processes, she could will her body to perform as she envisioned. To Helen, the only value she placed on her basketball days was learning how to work with and through her body. Despite being an "All Star," the important thing to her was the practical application in her life.

Helen also did not easily get along with anything mechanical. This was especially true with things that served no creative purpose in her life or that she was forced to learn or use. When she was about fifteen, her father tried to teach her to drive, and, she ran into the same learning problem. Her father explained to her the principles of driving and then showed her by the example of driving himself. However, she was terrified of driving. She said that first she had to overcome this fear by making friends with the process of driving and then the car itself. She did this by allowing her feeling nature to embrace the car. In essence, she had to establish a relationship with it and then allow that relationship to teach her how to use it. Until this process took hold within her, she could not grasp even the fundamentals.

Once while driving around the farm with her father looking on, she almost knocked him down. This scared her even more and almost stopped her father from teaching her to drive altogether. However, they persisted, even though in the process she tore up a bridge behind the house and once ran off a field road into their house. During the next few years she said she had many more minor accidents before she finally came to peace with cars and driving. Helen had to have some compelling reason to learn how to relate to a physical world that often seemed foreign to her. She had to consciously use the same creative mind power and will she used to direct her physical body to learn how to use or direct anything of a material nature. And once again, when she put her mind to it, she could perform the task with much skill, knowledge and creativity.

This was also true with sewing and using a sewing machine. Helen valued her mother's creative sewing abilities and appreciated her passing these skills onto her. Sewing gave Helen a physical creative outlet into which her active mental activity could flow. She could visualize clothes and how they would look on herself or someone else before creating the vision. Through sewing she learned how to select materials, patterns and styles to express a particular feeling she wanted manifested in her life.

In her later spiritual work she called this "energy qualification." For Helen, the process of designing and creating clothes to express some personal essence or an image was no different from an architect designing and creating a building for a particular effect. Both are innovative activities that are essential to conscious, creative life. She inherently connected with her inner resources and directed them through her various creative projects. To Helen, learning to create conscious "thought forms" was part of becoming a co-creator with God. She actively used this developed ability to serve God's Plan throughout her life.

# PART TWO:

# IN SEARCH OF FREEDOM

*Frederick R. Kipp*

# Chapter One

At thirteen, Helen was sent home from school for letting a boy kiss her. She was very naive as she entered her teenage years and didn't know what to do when a boy tried to kiss her. Seeing nothing wrong with trying this new experience, she allowed it. The consequences were immediate and drastic. The school principal acted severely, and her parents' reaction further damaged their already strained relationship. It was clear her parents were more concerned about what others thought rather than what happened or how Helen felt about it.

Although disappointed by her mother's reaction, she was devastated by her father's. He told her "People will think you're a whore for letting a boy kiss you." He berated and degraded her to the point that she felt dirty and unhappy with herself. In her heart she knew that she had done nothing to warrant such extreme reaction and condemnation. If this was what it felt like to be humiliated, she certainly didn't want to judge or condemn others for anything. The whole experience was so devastating that it strengthened her resolve to get away from home as soon as she was old enough.

After all she suffered over the kissing incident, little did she know that later the same boy would ask her to marry him. Johnnie Ferrell Parrish was only fifteen at the time, but apparently he knew his mind and the girl he wanted. At the time, Helen suspected she would marry him someday. However, at thirteen she just couldn't cope with the thought of marriage to anyone. As they dated and she got closer to finishing high school, she began to accept the inevitability that they would marry.

When asked what Ferrell was like, Helen smiled with great warmth and with a sparkle in her eyes, and said, "He was very good looking; you know, the strong silent type of man." Even though Helen was outwardly friendly and personable, she felt more comfortable as an introvert. She liked long periods of silence within her own thoughts and enjoyed just being with someone without exchanging a word. So she liked his quiet ways and his strength made her feel protected. However, later she found out there were some definite drawbacks to his silence.

Once while they were dating in high school, Ferrell did not show up for a date. This was unusual and he never phoned to say why. He went through the whole summer without seeing or talking to Helen. Later that year, he just showed up at the house one day and asked her out. Although he never told her why he broke that date, Helen knew from other sources that his car had broken down and his brother Glenn and his wife would not let him borrow their car.

21

He was very loyal to his brother and never spoke a word against him. In this situation he was so embarrassed by Glenn's refusal that he could not face Helen. The fact that Ferrell was more concerned with his own reaction and his brother's feelings than with hers always troubled Helen and made her later question her trust in him and his loyalty to her.

Throughout their early relationship, Helen constantly heard from family, friends and neighbors about Ferrell's friendly personality, his sense of humor and his wit. She saw this in his relationship with his mother, her father and her sister's husband. Ferrell seemed to have a special kind of bond with them. Although a man of few words with Helen, Ferrell had many good friendships and enjoyed other people. Helen felt hurt that he didn't feel comfortable enough around her to reveal this lighter side of himself and she wasn't sure why.

Another surprise about Ferrell was that his relationship with Glenn was not all it seemed to be. Despite Ferrell's loyalty to his brother, Helen discovered that he had a history of conflict with him. A few years after they were married, Ferrell's mother told her how difficult it was for him to live in his older brother's shadow. Glenn considered himself superior to Ferrell in all respects and never missed an opportunity to remind him of this. Apparently he did so by criticizing everything Ferrell did and said. At the time, Ferrell's deep and bitter resentment of Glenn came as quite a shock to Helen, but later it made perfect sense. It explained the tension she had always felt between the brothers but could not identify.

A few months after Helen graduated from high school in 1950, Ferrell joined the Navy and went for basic training to the US Naval Training Center in Great Lakes, Illinois. After completing basic training in December, he came home to Tennessee on leave before reporting to his first duty station in Corpus Christi, Texas. The day after Christmas he asked Helen to marry him - well, almost asked. As Helen tells the story, they were sitting on the sofa talking and he said, "will you" then abruptly stopped talking. Without thinking, Helen finished his sentence for him by saying, "marry me?" He replied "yes" and she said "yes," and the next day they drove to Corinth, Mississippi where they were married.

This was not an easy time for either of them. Although they had agreed to marry, Helen feared that they each wanted to marry just to get away from home. It was as if neither could achieve this escape by themselves but together it seemed possible. She was concerned that their mutual desire to get out of town might not be the best way to start a marriage. Also, it seemed that Ferrell's basic nature was well suited to life in Medina which made her worry that he might not be happy elsewhere. Hearing later of Ferrell's difficulty with his brother helped to relieve her concerns and to more fully clarify why he wanted to escape with her. Helen knew exactly why she had to leave and was determined to find her freedom somewhere. She said that although she really loved Ferrell, these concerns gave her doubts about marrying him. On their drive home from Corinth, she couldn't help wondering if they would make it and just how long it might take to find out.

In early January 1951, only a week or so after their wedding, Ferrell left for Texas without her. He went ahead to report for duty and to find them a place to live. When Helen arrived in early February, their living situation was still unsettled because the Navy had not approved the apartment Ferrell had rented. This immediately made it necessary to find another place to live. She was free of her parents and Medina but her new beginning was anything but smooth. Those first few months of married life in Corpus Christi must have been like a bad dream. They were newlyweds and neither had ever been on their own before. Shortly after moving into their second apartment, the building complex was raided by the police for drugs. As it turned out, it was a mistake because the building across the street was the one to be raided. Their inexperience made finding a decent but affordable place to live quite difficult on their Navy housing allowance.

During their first year together they moved several more times. Each new place had its own peculiar problems that made it difficult to settle into any kind of routine. But in time they found ways to create a life together. Helen soon found work as a clerk and load dispatcher for the Corpus Christi Central Power & Light Company. One day, while working, she saw a man electrocuted in the high-voltage electrical equipment yard. Apparently he was a daredevil type who got careless and paid the price with his life. After getting over the initial horror of the scene, she managed to turn this traumatic event into a positive learning experience. In her own way, she also had a daredevil side to her nature. This had always frightened her and had made her seem wild to others. Although her spirit felt enlivened by this energy, she had no intention of letting it kill her. She writes, "Although I believe wholeheartedly in God's protection, He cannot protect me from myself - stupidity can get me killed."

Also while working for the power company, she met a man in the office who provided her with another learning opportunity. This man had lost both arms in an electrical work accident. As they got to know one another, he shared with her that even though he lost his arms he could still feel them. After the accident his doctors told him that this sensation would go away in time. However, it had been several years by then and the feeling was still there. To her surprise, she believed the man was really feeling his arms and wondered how this could be.

Helen thought on this question and took it to God many times before she received an unusual and unexpected form of help. One day as she thought about the man and held his image in her mind's eye, he began to look out of focus. Each frame of him, so to speak, had a complete body including arms and legs superimposed over one another. As this vision continued, she began to realize that she was seeing a part or dimension of his being that went beyond his physical form. Invisible to physical eyesight, she later learned she was viewing his subtle energy bodies.

Naively she had always thought her childhood experiences were just her own. However, if what she saw in this man was accurate, she realized she was way over her head, and that her private unseen realm might very well be impersonal and universal. Until this experience, her understanding of the external world was governed by what she was taught in school and church. Seeing this man's etheric body caused her private unseen world to merge with her external reality. This was fascinating but frightening to her at the same time.

Unfortunately, she wouldn't find any written material to help make sense of the experience for almost ten years. In retrospect, Helen saw that this was her next step into a new way of learning. Through the struggle to understand, her perspective of reality changed to help her better understand the visible world and validated her earlier spiritual experiences in the invisible world. This increased her self-confidence and laid a foundation for future inner exploration.

Towards the end of their first year together, life in Corpus Christi stabilized. They made new friends, shared some activities together and were learning how to relate to one another. When they first married, Ferrell rarely spoke with her about anything. At first, this allowed Helen to enjoy her own internal solitude. After a while, though, she wanted more communication and personal interaction with him. However, when she brought things up to talk about, mostly he ignored her or gave a minimal response. Although this concerned her, she let it go by, focusing on her appreciation of the many ways he gave her freedom to be herself. This was in direct contrast to her father, who believed he had the right to command Helen to act and live the way he wanted. She truly appreciated Ferrell for this accommodation.

Sometime later, Ferrell became a little more expressive with Helen. But the more verbal he became, the more demanding he was in his behavior towards her. During their first year together, Helen gained some weight. Ferrell didn't like the way she looked and frequently scolded her about it. Finally he told her she should take up smoking to help her lose weight. This was a complete turnaround for him because in the past every time he saw a woman smoking he commented negatively about it. To placate him and under his direction, she began smoking. As it turned out, it did help her lose weight and she even found it enjoyable because it was something she could share with Ferrell. However, on their next visit to Medina she saw a side of Ferrell's personality that troubled her deeply.

One day while visiting his family, he came into a room where Helen was smoking while chatting with others. He walked straight over to where she was sitting, hit her on the head and told her it didn't look good for her to smoke. She felt humiliated. Although the blow was not all that hard, the fact that he did it at all hurt her deeply. This single incident probably did more to damage their relationship than anything else up to that point. In his own way, Ferrell was becoming very much like her father. As he felt more confident in their relationship, his subdued behavior was giving way to a more aggressive part of him that inherently claimed the right to control her life.

Helen was long-suffering when difficulties arose with others. She seemed to silently change herself rather than to cause a scene or unpleasantness for other people. This apparent lack of self-defense often led others to assume her accommodation to them had no limits. However, she did have limits and reached them very quickly when people tried to control her. When that happened, she just bided her time until she was able or ready to act, and act she did!

As time went on, other problems arose between her and Ferrell that troubled her. Helen learned that she could not share with him her interpretations of situations or events in their life nor her perceptions of people they knew. When she did he became very disturbed and, in some cases, he even accused her of making it up or of being crazy. Because of this she had to withdraw a large part of herself from him and their relationship.

In November of that year, she went to see a doctor with a sore stomach. After the examination the doctor told her that she needed an appendectomy. For some reason Helen suspected that her appendix was not the problem and mentioned it to her doctor. Immediately she was sorry that she did because he got angry and sternly told her not to interfere in things she knew nothing about. After the operation she asked to see the appendix. It was plain to all who saw it that there was nothing wrong with it, but the doctor refused to talk about the subject again. This incident began her mistrust of doctors and the medical profession because it assumed an indisputable authority over her that she could not accept.

Another aspect of this experience that added to her mistrust was her discovery she did not respond well to anesthesia. While being anesthetized, Helen suddenly and uncontrollably started fighting to get off the table. In doing so, she hit a nurse hard enough to give her a black eye and it took several people to hold her down until she finally became unconscious. Besides being very sick while coming out from under the anesthesia, she also had to be restrained. Everyone, including Ferrell, regarded her as "the problem" rather than it being caused by an adverse drug reaction. Generally, this was a very traumatic experience for Helen and as a result, she decided never be anesthetized or take any drug again.

This hospital event seemed to push Helen and Ferrell further apart. He just couldn't seem to get over his embarrassment and remained upset with her for her behavior in the hospital. Helen said that it so unnerved him he couldn't even begin to discuss it without getting upset all over again. She always felt that in this incident he saw the part of her nature and spirit that he could not control. As difficulties between them increased, Helen began to suspect that she would never be the kind of wife Ferrell sincerely wanted and genuinely needed to be happy. It was possible, she believed, that he too began to see this because afterwards he became distant and withdrawn again.

Ferrell's inability to cope with an independent Helen became more evident as time passed. His behavior increasingly convinced her that she could expect no genuine support from him. When difficulties arose between them, Ferrell isolated himself and forced Helen to deal with them alone. Theirs was not turning into the marriage relationship she wished for them, and she began to accept that she was truly on her own. As a result, she never really felt secure with Ferrell again. She said, "When things didn't go the way he expected, he fell to pieces and it was up to me to pull myself through." Feeling as though she had no other choice, she decided to learn how to live her life with, but independently of, Ferrell.

# Chapter Two

In 1952 the Navy assigned Ferrell to a ship for sea duty. While away, as Helen put it, "He delivered me and the car to his mother in Medina, Tennessee for safe keeping." So here she was back where she began, but she was definitely not the same person who had left. The next two years increased her need for change and freedom even more.

At first, Helen lived with Ferrell's mother and grandmother. This lasted for about a year before she moved to her own place. Both women were very kind to her and upon her arrival made her feel very much at home. She really enjoyed getting to know Ferrell's mother and they had many pleasant talks while she lived with them. For the first time Helen felt as if she had someone who would really listen to her. However, she began to realize that Ferrell's mother was sharing the content of these talks with her mother as well as with Glenn's wife. Helen felt hurt by this breach of her confidence. She did not realize that by living in this house she had entered into a kind of female, family hierarchy, with herself at the bottom. To make matters worse, Glenn's wife used every opportunity to put Helen in her place and to speak about Helen to the other women behind her back.

Although in many ways difficult, the challenges of this period forced her to grow up and to define herself apart from her family and the area identity. Helen was a quick study and before long found ways to work around the pain and conflict caused by her living conditions. Pain was to become one of Helen's most proficient teachers in life. To release it, she had to look at herself and others with objectivity and clarity. She also learned to move decisively and efficiently through her own internal inertia and that which she met in people around her.

As a child Helen developed a simple internal process to deal with problems using the imagery of God's golden throne, as taught in church. She writes about it as follows:

"At night, when things were difficult in school or any problem in my life seemed insurmountable, I imagined that God lifted me up and set me on the steps beside His throne. From that place I talked to Him about my problems. He didn't exactly give me answers but rather He asked me to look back and find the planet earth. At first all I could see was a mass of stars. This meant that He had to direct me to the earth. It looked just like all the other millions of lights in space. Then He would ask me to find the area where I lived on the planet. Again, I needed His help finding that area on earth. After all this He would ask me what my problem was again. Something always changed in me because, at that point, my problems didn't seem so important in the overall scheme of the universe. I began to see that everything was a matter of perception and that my problems were as big or as small as I wanted them to be. As I sat there and looked at them from that perspective, a release always came from inside my body and usually I dropped off to sleep. When I awakened in the morning, the situation was probably just the same, but I didn't feel the frustration or hysteria over it."

Later she learned that God was all around her and that she no longer had to go anywhere in particular to get understanding and release. So anywhere she was, in her mind, she just pulled herself up into the corner of a room and looked down from there on the situation and the people involved. Again she writes:

"From that high vantage point I found that I didn't understand others any better than they understood me. From that perspective I asked God to help me understand the situation and the viewpoints of all the people involved. This did not always take away the pain. However, when I crawled down from that corner of the room I knew I had to let go of my feelings to the point where I wasn't upset anymore with the others over the situation."

Much later in life Helen realized it was through simple self-initiated rituals as these that she learned how to rise in consciousness or meditate automatically to find immediate answers or release. (Helen always had a way of making things seem very easy and simple. Doing what she describes, however, is not as easy as it sounds. It takes a considerable amount of will, focus and persistence to go instantaneously into a state of meditative prayer regardless of the pressures or distractions in the environment.)

In January 1953, Helen went to work as a production clerk for a shoe manufacturer in Milan, Tennessee. She worked for this company until the factory closed in April 1956. This job provided an income to support her living on her own. If she was going to be independent, she knew she needed more practical experience with all types of situations and people in the world. One area in particular that troubled her was that of gender barriers and discrimination. In 1953, a highly spirited twenty-one-year-old woman was someone to be stifled, not encouraged. Helen said that although she was in many respects still naive, she had a stable sense of self, was self-reliant and expected fair and equal treatment by all. This led many men mistakenly to believe that she felt herself superior to them which encouraged them to put her in her place.

Helen observed other women in her life who acted in an inferior manner and deferred to men outwardly, but inwardly collectively joined in a type of moral superiority. She learned that this gave them justification and support for controlling and manipulating men behind the scenes. Because freedom was essential to Helen, in good conscience she could not try to control or manipulate anyone, male or female. As a result of this attitude, she found the interpersonal dynamics of work and socializing very tedious and tiring. She refused to assume roles or behavior that were not compatible with her own convictions.

Life and work were very difficult and there were times when she questioned her commitment to live her independent ideals so actively. All she met was resistance and she couldn't understand why. Then, she came across a booklet that helped to change the way she looked at herself and others. It was entitled "What You See in Others Is What You Are." She writes:

"I don't think I even read the booklet. It was on the top of the newsstand and just seeing the title made a lasting impression on me. Immediately I believed the essence of the message and started applying it to myself. At first I didn't think it fit me too well and there were times when I was sure it didn't and got so angry that I saw red! I didn't like believing that I could be like some of the bitches and bastards I ran across - I couldn't possibly have that kind of energy in me. When something about another person made me angry, I was certain what I saw was not inside me. Sometimes it took me weeks to work around to facing that I did have it."

Everything she learned as theory, she applied relentlessly to herself. Once she embraced the truth of a situation, she incorporated what she learned into her life. In many ways this growth came at the expense of her sense of self when she developed too much understanding and deference to others. Because so many people misunderstood her, automatically she gave everyone else the benefit of the doubt and honestly tried to understand others from their point of view. Once she assessed why they believed and acted the way they did, she was able to make room for them, as they were, inside herself.

This definitely caused her problems. In giving others freedom, many people mistakenly thought that they could control her. She knew there had to be a way to balance being true to herself while at the same time being understanding of others; she just had to find it. The way, she learned, wasn't easy or painless because when she stood her ground, even gently, it upset people. Despite this type of reaction, for the next ten years Helen honestly and earnestly applied what she learned to improve herself and the quality of her life. With a lot of internal struggle during this period, her personality developed and matured as she further defined her commitment to growth and moved towards greater freedom in her life.

With her return to Medina, Helen began going to church again, this time to one of her own choosing. After her earlier church experiences with both parents, this was an important decision and action for her to take. She began to realize that both church experiences were so traumatic that at times the memory of them plunged her into periods of religious disillusionment. She was always grateful, though, that she managed to get free of both churches. As she worked through these old memories, she learned that behind the emotionalism in her mother's church, there were true spiritual feelings within herself and in the other members. In her father's church, she learned to think about religion and life with an open mind. In retrospect, she said that each experience gave her much self-understanding and growth that otherwise she would have missed.

# Chapter Three

When Ferrell returned home from the Navy in 1954, Helen was not the same person he left in safekeeping with his mother, but neither was he. Helen felt his military experience somehow left him feeling happy to return to life in Medina and he seemed more comfortable with the area and with the people. This concerned her because she began to suspect that he no longer shared their goal of getting away and feared that they might be back in Medina for good.

After his return, Ferrell was unemployed for six months. Even though Helen was working to support them, he assumed an attitude of carrying their relationship. She endured this period comforted by her belief that he needed time to adjust to civilian life and that once he got a job things would be better for them. Ferrell's attitude did not change and married life grew more difficult for Helen. After Ferrell went to work, he did little to help her with the responsibilities of maintaining their household and life together. From a much later perspective, Helen said he wasn't really any different from any other man of that time and was simply following the male conditioning of the day. Helen felt certain that her new sense of independence threatened him. However, understanding this did not make his attitude and behavior towards her any easier to accept.

It was not Helen's nature to be a complainer. If she did not like something, she spoke about it directly. Having done that, she rarely mentioned it again and continued to live her life without further comment. However, it was a mistake for anyone to think that because she dropped something, she had forgotten about it. She always gave others more than enough time to consider her viewpoint. If no joint resolution came within what she considered more than a reasonable time, she simply moved ahead independently. Usually this meant internal self-changes as a precursor to external changes that affected the people involved. This silent preparation for action could, at times, leave people feeling blindsided. When she finally acted, she was direct and honest in her behavior. She would not accept treatment or behavior from others that was unjust or demeaning, nor did she feel it her responsibility to force anyone to change or to do anything against their will.

Ferrell was an avid sportsman, a loyal St. Louis Cardinals baseball fan and he loved Guy Lombardo music. He mostly read sports magazines and liked listening to baseball on the radio or watching a televised game. Sometimes he did both simultaneously. They really didn't share many activities and practically speaking, lived separate lives.

Most of their social activity involved Ferrell's brother, Glenn, and his wife. Often on weekends, they joined them for fishing at a cabin on the Tennessee River that Ferrell and Glenn built together. Helen found the silence of early morning fishing quite enjoyable. While being around the others, it gave her time for her own thoughts and an opportunity to share something quietly with Ferrell that he really enjoyed. This was a rarity for them and she took every opportunity she could find to share his life and interests. Even though Helen was a part of these weekend trips, she did not feel truly included. The other three seemed to relate easily and freely but Helen felt her presence made them feel uncomfortable. When she tried to join in their conversations, she met a wall of silence.

She never looked forward to their drive home from these weekends. Ferrell's brooding silence always left her feeling as if she had done something to ruin his weekend. It seemed that the real difficulty between them was facing the painful reality that they were growing apart and that apparently there was nothing either of them could do about it.

Although Helen had friendly relations with people from work and church, none were close. Her sisters lived nearby, but she wasn't close to them either. Helen attributed this lack of intimacy to their differing childhood experiences. In contrast to their strained and distant relationship with Helen, her parents seemed to have a loving and personal relationship with her sisters. This led to much misunderstanding between them and prevented them from bonding in the traditional sisterly ways. Helen was treated like the "odd one out," which did not motivate her to share much of herself or her inner life with any of them. This turned out to be a wise decision since she learned later that her father had joined with his brother-in-law in committing his sister to a state mental institution. He did this simply because she spoke of what Helen considered similar experiences to her own!

Despite Helen's love for her family, it was not enough to bridge the widening differences between them. Ferrell, on the other hand was becoming closer to his family, and this increased their sense of growing apart. To make matters worse, Ferrell regularly took sides against her in family matters or disagreements. Here again, she was treated as the odd one out with little hope of receiving respect as an individual in her marriage, or from either family. Eventually Helen did come to peace with her family difficulties when she saw how they helped set the stage for her path of individuation and separation from her social and cultural conditioning.

By late 1957, Helen was desperate for a major change in her life. Something had to give and to her surprise it was Glenn who made it possible. He worked for a government contractor and had access to circulars about government job openings around the country. Glenn gave Helen a flyer about a general clerk's position at the Army Ballistic Missile Agency (later to become NASA's Marshall Space Flight Center) at Redstone Arsenal in Huntsville, Alabama.

Glenn's goodwill gesture caught her off guard. She found herself wondering if this was his way of getting her out of the picture so that she and Ferrell might divorce. It really didn't matter though because she was deeply grateful to have something to check out away from the Medina area. She applied for the job, got it and prepared to move to Huntsville. This was the change for which she had been waiting and she was ready to act. Conditions were such in her marriage that she really didn't care whether Ferrell joined her or not.

# Chapter Four

In preparing for the move to Alabama, Ferrell's attitude and behavior surprised Helen. Not only did he join her, he did everything he could to assist and support her. So, in a reversal of their move to Texas, Helen left for Alabama in February 1958 to start her new job and to find a place for them to live. Ferrell joined her a few months later. Upon arriving in Huntsville, Ferrell seemed more agreeable and in much better spirits than before. Looking back, Helen suspected that he too was ready to get away from Medina and the family but just didn't know how to talk about it or what to do. Not long after his arrival, Ferrell started work at the US Army Missile Command where he worked for the next seven years.

To Helen, Huntsville was a welcome relief. The focus of the emerging space and technology industry gave the traditional southern culture a progressive and worldly atmosphere. She met people from all parts of the United States and some from foreign countries. At age twenty-six, Helen felt as if she was beginning a new life. Her spirit felt liberated and Huntsville represented an opportunity to live in the freedom of her own identity.

A month after starting her new job as a general lab clerk, she was promoted to be secretary to the Lab Director, Hans Maus. Somehow, Mr. Maus saw something in Helen that others had missed. From the time Helen became his secretary he treated her with respect and believed in her capabilities and potential. He played an important part in her professional life for the next ten years. The very part of Helen's spirit that others found challenging and uncontrollable, he appreciated and encouraged to its fullest expression. From the start, Helen felt comfortable in the presence of so many innovative thinkers. For years she had pushed the envelope of her creative mind in search of new ways of looking at herself and the world. She felt stifled by the restraints of rural Tennessee life but now found herself in a place and environment that continued to challenge her and stimulate her need to keep expanding herself and her mind.

Some years before, a doctor told Helen she could never have children. Apparently her reproductive system had never matured beyond the biological age of thirteen. So you can imagine her shock when shortly after moving to Huntsville she started experiencing the symptoms of pregnancy. She went to a doctor who treated her condescendingly for even thinking she might be pregnant. He told her that her ovaries and uterus were so small that pregnancy was impossible. Even though humiliated by the doctor's response and treatment, she knew her body and asked him to test her. Reluctantly, he ordered a pregnancy test. Although he never apologized for his behavior towards her, the results showed that Helen was pregnant.

Neither she nor Ferrell could have imagined they would ever have a child, as this was supposed to be a medical impossibility. For Helen, the birth of their son, Jeffery, on January 6, 1959 was the miracle that confirmed for her that all things are possible in God - even if the human world doesn't think so. This was an important lesson for Helen. Through it she learned to trust completely the power of God to change anything, even the matter of her body! Jeffery's birth was a gift of immense significance to Helen and it made finding her own freedom even more important. Freedom was everything to Helen, and as a parent she could think of nothing more valuable to pass on to her son than the Spirit of Freedom.

With Jeffery's birth, both she and Ferrell found a new and common purpose in their relationship. Jeffery seemed to bring out the tender and loving side of Ferrell and for the first time in their marriage he seemed genuinely happy. It was as if Ferrell found new vitality in life by being a father. He was even receptive to Helen's suggestion that they join a church. This was the first time in Helen's memory that he had ever shown any interest in religion or church. They were proud parents as their son was christened a few months later, witnessed by their family and friends, in the Medina Methodist Church. They were a family now and bought their first house together to settle more deeply into their life in Huntsville.

Helen felt strongly that Jeffery had a particular spiritual destiny to fulfill. As a living example to him, it was time for her to find her own and to learn to live it. She writes, "I began to rethink life and my determination to find my own identity - Jeffery's birth started this process in me." She began reading and studying all the great religions, psychology, philosophy, metaphysics, science and self-help books. All the new ideas began to enrich her understanding of life. As a result, she started to realize that in the overall scheme of things it really didn't matter to which belief system, religion or discipline one subscribed. Every human life was a path to the truth of God. To Helen, all that mattered was making a choice and commitment, then God would do the rest.

Helen's awareness of the multiple dimensions of life continued to increase after Jeffery's birth. She could not explain her inner experiences to herself, let alone to anyone else. She often said that if she hadn't lived them herself, she would have had a hard time believing them real. They were real, but how and why? First, she decided, she needed to find out what the world knew that might help to explain them to her. Religion hadn't provided any reasonable answers so perhaps science could. In her new environment, she found considerable compatibility between her own self-taught thinking processes and the scientific method of thought. Rather than applying this method to understanding the world of tangible objects, she applied it to herself and her experiences to try to bring balance and meaning to her existence. This perspective made her working environment even more compelling.

When she arrived in Huntsville she could not have imagined the life changes this move would initiate. At the time, it was enough for her to know that she was moving in some direction. Movement towards change and transformation was important to her and she began to appreciate the willful, driving part of her psyche and the crucial role its purposeful direction played in keeping her life dynamically alive. After seeing the words "what you see in others is what you are," Helen's internal life was never the same. This message continued to work on her as she internalized its truth. She knew she felt driven to do something more with herself and life, but what? Somewhere deep inside she knew her literal survival depended on following the impulse to change, no matter where it took her.

As far as she knew at the time, she had no life-threatening illness and she was not in any other physical danger. So why did she feel that her life depended on this insistent and persistent need to change? To Helen, all people are called to do something in life and they cannot reasonably or adequately explain to anyone why or how they know it. They just know that for some reason their sense of physical, psychological or spiritual survival depends on following that inner impulse to wherever it leads them. She believed and understood that all people are called by God to live the lives they lead. Call it karma, divine guidance, ego or necessity, but it is still a calling. Life leads us into the experiences we need, individually as humans and jointly as humanity, to continue to grow and evolve in consciousness to know more of God and to fulfill our destiny. She liked to call the point where one first consciously contacts this driving and guiding force as "Having your number called by God."

For Helen, change was accelerating from many directions simultaneously. It seemed as if the move, the new job, and the miracle of Jeffery's birth all came together as her "number call." This catapulted her from her active but internal orientation of change, to an external one that increasingly affected all of their lives. She tried to contain the effects of her internal changes but this was becoming more difficult. Life without the freedom to find and fulfill her purpose in God was meaningless and unlivable. But it was also important to her to preserve the stability of her family life.

The path of transformation is tedious and grueling and Helen struggled with the same psychological and practical challenges as any woman of her age. She had to work at integrating her insights and revelations into her everyday life and personality. She wrote:

"By the time I was about 30, I had tried to put into practice everything I had learned in my study of life, but I felt as if none of it was getting me anywhere. I didn't like being one person for my husband, then another for my boss and a different person for everyone else. I knew what pleased each - I could be it, but I didn't like it. I wanted to be happy with myself, so something more in me had to change. It wasn't that I wanted to make anyone unhappy, I just wanted to find my own identity apart from others. I especially hated being expected to do housework or other domestic duties simply because I was a woman. This was a real pressurized time for me and I went through a long and difficult struggle over these things before I got to this point. So I went and stood in the corner of my bedroom. I said to God you can strike me dead but I do not believe what I've been taught about life or how I've been taught to live. I am going to start being me! I am not trying to hurt anybody but I must find out what I think and want to do, not what somebody else wants me to do."

This sounds like a simple declaration to make, but it isn't. It takes courage to stand before God and proclaim that you are wiping the slate clean of everything you learned to accept about life and mean it. Helen thoroughly believed that if what she was saying or was about to do did not please God, He would tell her immediately. This was the depth and power of her God reality. Her desperation was real and so was her commitment to devote herself completely to living and acting on her own interpretations of God and life, whatever the personal cost.

Several years of reevaluating, rethinking and reprogramming her life were necessary to make this brief declaration a reality. It was a rough road for her and all those in her life. In another section of her writing she says:

"It was hard on me. I did not conform to collective expectations and agreements and no one liked it. Because what I was doing affected others they were upset about it and it was easy to slip back into my old habits. Every time I did, I couldn't stand myself until I corrected this and went back to being true to myself. This did not always make me popular and boy how I wished I didn't have to be myself. However, I couldn't live without knowing how I thought and felt about everything. When I found out what I really thought about everything and developed the courage to be that - many times I found out that it really wasn't too important."

This may sound as if she went through an awful lot of unpleasantness and trouble for nothing but that is not how she saw it. Every step or action she took caused internal chaos to begin some shift within her. When she came out at the other end, she had transformed some aspect of herself, from the inside out. Helen gained considerable personal power from going into the depths of her unconscious world to see if she liked what was there. By initiating steps to change what she didn't like, she worked to make her life her own by reclaiming her identity from past conditioning. As a result, she felt stronger and transformed by the experience. The power of self-knowledge is something that no one can challenge or take away.

# Chapter Five

Everything about life in Huntsville affected Helen deeply. She discovered that creating a new life based on her own conscious identity disrupted everything in her life. It stimulated movement towards change in many directions and dimensions at the same time. However, the time was right for her to step up the process of breaking free from the identity and life imposed upon her by her past. She had earnestly tried to live the values she was taught earlier in her life. This did not work because it was too full of limitation. Internally she still struggled against the unconscious patterns she accepted from her family, church and community life. If she was to fulfill her purpose in God, whatever that was, it was God's energy that she must live and embody.

The four years after Jeffery's birth were hard but productive for Helen. She used these years to set consciously, deep within herself, the seeds of her future life. During that period she found her identity while at the same time deciding it was not enough. As a result, Helen accelerated her self-examination and worked to be more aggressive in applying what she learned. But Helen was not an outwardly aggressive person. At times, she could almost seem passive and withdrawn from the world around her. Where many people sort out their lives and define themselves through external activity, Helen preferred a quiet, internal focus. This could often look as if she was indecisive and slow to act. However, once she was satisfied with her internal changes and foundation, she moved forward decisively and with incredible speed.

Helen continued to concentrate and reflect on the message "what you see in others is what you are." She wanted to know where these elusive parts lived within her and how they got there without her knowing it. In her reading on psychology she found some answers to these questions in the description and definition of the subconscious and unconscious mind. It was exhilarating to find an entire discipline that provided a structure and definition for her interests and questions. This information gave her a considerable new direction for continued work on herself. However, still she struggled with the idea that there were parts of herself of which she was unaware. It troubled her that these parts might be compelling her to behave in ways contrary to her intentions and wishes.

In the early sixties, Helen came across two theories. They were reincarnation (the belief that the Soul returns after death and is reborn into consecutive embodiments or incarnations), and teleportation (the ability to move a person or thing from one location to another by dematerialization and then rematerialization). After learning about these theories, she thought them to be true but did not know them to be true. She always went through her own process of verification before she could say she knew something to be true, but only for herself.

Reincarnation, and its principles of karma (the law of cause and effect), offered Helen possible answers to many more of her unanswered questions about, for example, the Christian doctrine of original sin and why seemingly innocent children die so early in their life. These had always bothered her. In addition, she was always troubled by the idea that she only had one life in which to get into heaven. To Helen this was neither logical nor consistent with her experience of natural life being a dynamic ongoing process of birth, death and renewal, rather than a single event. With these new theories to explore, her internal thought process and inner spiritual realm greatly expanded in depth and scope. She found that her early childhood experiences with the Holy Spirit had prepared her well to experience and be receptive to the nonphysical realities of life. Her experiences of feeling, transported back to earlier times and events in history, now made sense to her as an adult.

However, nothing to date had prepared her for what happened next. Suddenly, uninvited and without warning, people from other dimensions started showing up to talk. This she did not welcome and she always felt psychically invaded when it happened. To find out what was going on she spoke with them and discovered they were dead people who just wanted to speak through her with their living relatives. One of these people was a young man with whom she had worked and who had recently died. He asked her to get in touch with his mother to let her know that he was all right. To help him, she agreed to contact his mother but the result was only to upset the man's mother. Having to face the reactions in others through these communications was more trouble to Helen than it was worth. She got so thoroughly irritated with these disembodied people showing up in her meditations and thoughts, that she wanted them to go away and never to talk to her again.

This was not an easy thing to do and it took many hours and days of hard work and focus of will to accomplish it. As a result of these experiences, though, she learned how to begin to create safeguards and protections to keep these entities from invading her life in the future. Through this she also learned the value of developing discrimination to help her know with whom to speak in the vast range and hierarchy of energies and beings.

Helen's inner life experiences started to become just as real and ordinary as anything in the outer material world. This was not something she could stop at will. When God chose to speak with her or to show her something, there was no peace until she listened or watched. Most people have natural, protective barriers (called etheric webs) between the spiritual and material worlds. However, either Helen did not have these barriers at birth or she broke through them early on in her life. It really didn't matter how it happened because the fact was that now she was unable to keep these two worlds separate and apart.

Helen was quite pleased when a friend recommended to her a set of books entitled "Teachings of the Masters of the Far East." Reading these books had a profound impact on her. According to accounts in these books, there were beings called "Ascended Masters." They were evolved beings from an inner Spiritual Hierarchy of God who were in service for a particular time to help direct, teach and protect humanity and the earth. The books told of particular Masters who taught how to raise the energy level in the physical body so that it did not have to go through the process of death. The purpose of this teaching was to make what is called a "physical ascension." As described, this meant passing directly into the next and higher energy vibration of life while simultaneously dematerializing the physical body to ascend into a newer, more subtle or refined level of matter. It further reported that once in that ascended state these Masters could rematerialize their physical bodies so that people could see and touch them.

The message and promise contained within these books resonated within Helen's heart and mind. Something "clicked" inside her and suddenly her experiences with the seen and unseen dimensions of life came into clearer focus and took on new meaning. With the possibility of this ascended life, she began to see other possible answers to her remaining scriptural and philosophical questions about all life and its deeper purpose. However, she realized that there was a vast gulf between thinking or even believing ascension possible and actually accomplishing it. It did not suddenly happen simply because one believed it possible. She had to find out for herself how it was done. This new information also made the theory of teleportation plausible to her. If one could consciously learn to increase the vibration of the physical body to be compatible with existence on these higher levels or planes without dying, then it seemed possible to dematerialize and rematerialize the body at will.

The stories in this book, as well as ones she heard later, about times and places where these Masters transmitted their energy and wisdom through dictations, were amazing indeed. However, she had yet to meet someone in a physical body who had ascended. So, although she believed the accounts in these books to be true, she withheld judgment as to the practical possibility for herself until she had more personal information.

Helen often spoke of her relationship with a psychic, "the old man" as she called him, in Arab, Alabama. She found him to be a fellow student of life, an attentive listener with a brilliant mind, and someone with whom she could share her inner life. Although he did a few readings for her, this was not the main focus of their relationship. In essence, he was her first spiritual teacher. He assisted her in continuing to open and develop her own psychic faculties and introduced her to ancient esoteric wisdom and metaphysical principles through various books he recommended. This helped her to gain a much needed balance between her temporal and spiritual life.

It was also during this time that one of the Ascended Masters of the Far East, the Master Morya, began talking to her. The first few times, he appeared while she was meditating. At first she thought he was just another disembodied being or discarnate, so she immediately rejected his advances and tried to send him away. However, he persisted and did not leave. Finally, she began talking with him. As it turned out, his explanations of what was happening in her life were quite accurate and helpful, and he became Helen's trusted inner teacher and friend for the next ten years.

With assistance from Morya, Helen began to distance herself from the old man psychic. She knew what he taught her about inner plane life was accurate and full of wisdom, but, Morya told her that, in time, she would surpass his knowledge and would move on. This proved to be true.

Helen's introduction to the Ascended Masters also changed her earlier Christian relationship with Jesus. Through her inner relationship with Morya, she was introduced to Jesus as one of the many Ascended Masters working to bring the powerful redeeming energy of Christ to humanity and the earth. This meant that she was finally able to reconcile the man Jesus with the Christ. With this new perspective, she embraced a more universal Christ aspect or energy in God as the redeeming energy available to all rather than as the personal savior of Christianity. In doing so, the profoundness of the life of Jesus in the world was enhanced for her. Although a significant man, Jesus was not the Christ but rather a human vehicle for the Christ's physical life expression on earth.

For Helen, just thinking about the possibilities of transcending death increased her will and strength to persevere in the guidance of the Holy Spirit. It was a pivotal point in her spiritual development. Although she had achieved a level of personal growth and internal independence, nothing in her worldly life seemed to have enough meaning for her. She felt challenged by her job, her role as a mother and her commitment to study, but somehow these were not enough. The possibility of transcending physical death however, was something that spoke to her Spirit and got her creative energies stimulated and moving. The only thing she knew for sure was that if this were possible, God would get her through it. To begin with, her psychological and biological conditioning had to be confronted and changed because it recognized death as being inevitable and inescapable. This was a huge undertaking!

While she awaited God to reveal how to begin this task, she continued initiating her own processes and rituals of internal transmutation. For the next year, she got up every morning at 4:15 a.m. to meditate. This was her time alone with God before Ferrell or Jeffery awakened and she began her rigorous daily routine. It was through this early morning ritual that she reconditioned, or requalified as she called it, her unconscious and conscious life to prepare herself to release the limitations of death in her body. It was her choice and she pursued this work with God in such a way that she had no one to blame but herself for whatever happened. If she failed, she knew it would be because she did not follow God's instruction thoroughly enough.

In Helen's reading and study, she often got more out of little booklets or brochures than lengthy books. This was because she learned that the power of words is not in their form but in the feeling or spirit they convey or invoke within oneself. Sometimes the most concise statements have the greatest impact. The idea for this came from a brochure she found that briefly described how to work with and condition the subconscious mind to cause real change in one's life. The brochure explained that intention to change through affirmation or taking action to change was not enough without a strong desire to change. Deep-seated feeling was the real basis of desire and the key to change.

The brochure went on to say that repetitive verbal affirmations without corresponding feelings were ineffective in causing change. The first meditative affirmation she constructed for herself was "There is good, there is beauty, I am beauty, I am Light, I am joy, I am without limitation, there is no death!" With each word she used and spoke, she created a vision and feeling to go with it and used these with the words. She did this until she could not only see effects in her body, but could feel them also. When she felt the cellular vibration they invoked in her body, she knew that change was in progress and it was just a matter of time until it expressed in her life. (This may seem very simple and easy to do, but most people give up long before it is anchored in place deeply enough for the energy of change to take over.)

Another way of looking at very condensed statements (or affirmations) is to view them as seed thoughts. For Helen, seed thoughts were words or phrases that succinctly expressed volumes of understanding. If one is willing to devote the time and energy to think about them to bring them inside, they explain themselves as they unfold and grow as seeds planted in the mind. Helen considered the excessive use of words a waste of time and energy for anyone who had any degree of thinking capacity. This was especially true if one was even slightly intuitive. She used words and short phrases as stepping stones or doorways into the limitless energy streams from God's mind. To Helen this is where all ideas and thoughts originate anyway. So if she could find the right word to unlock the door into these streams, they would fill her or anyone else with meaning and understanding.

Helen's internal reliance on God was increasing and growing stronger. However, it became necessary for her to know that this relationship was an active part of her external life also. She said that this was a period in which she was driven to know, at greater levels, that her faith in God was enough to surrender her physical life to Him.

To achieve this type of unconditional surrender, she used some very novel techniques. Helen needed to know without hesitation that God could change the dense physical matter of her body while protecting her from danger. Often when in deep internal crises over something needing change, she went into a room by herself and told God that something had to change for her to go on living. Starting in the farthest corner of the room she walked towards the door. As she did this, she told God that if He did not agree with her need to break free of whatever it was, then He should strike her dead before she reached the door. She was not tempting God nor did she want God to do anything for her. It was simply a potent affirmation that she would rather die trusting God than to live without this conviction. (Over the years, she used many rituals like this to anchor the energy of her faith right into the matter of her physical body. She believed that no thought, feeling or spiritual energy work was complete until it penetrated the various levels of the unconscious and subconscious conditioning to impact and change her physical body. She lived this daily as her reality.)

Prayer became more and more an essential part of Helen's daily life. She instantaneously and automatically prayed to God about everything and anything. To her it was just as important to her physical life as air or water. She needed to know continuously and completely that her faith in God working through her prayers was total and not corruptible by her subconscious. Helen did this by always placing herself in what she called "God's Divine Justice." To Helen this meant that she released herself and others to God's Will, not hers. She needed to know beyond doubt that her faith was enough to receive God's healing energy. It got to the point where each time she experienced some physical ailment or problem, without hesitation she turned to God for healing or resolution. Helen accepted that God could do anything. Always, she posed the question "Was she ready and able to receive what God could do in her life?" Again, she realized it was unreasonable for her to tempt death seriously unless she knew the answer to that essential question.

The incident in which she answered this question to her satisfaction was in September 1962. One day in her kitchen she was using a pressure cooker. There was a problem with it and while she was trying to fix it, it exploded, spraying very hot grease over the right side of her face and body. Immediately she began praying and talking to God asking for healing. This went on for the next two hours before she knew the burn was healed and she went on with her cooking. After the event it was difficult even to talk about it because there were no burns or blisters to prove to anyone that it had happened at all. Although it would have been helpful to have had Ferrell or someone else join her in her celebration of God's power it was not necessary. Helen knew what had happened and now knew that her faith was strong enough for God to intercede directly and change her physical body.

# Chapter Six

As 1963 began, Helen began to experience increasing clarity about the direction she should take in her life. In the five years following Jeffery's birth, she and Ferrell had settled into a type of mutually accommodating relationship. Other than Jeffery, they had few interests or activities in common. Although Ferrell was not actively supportive of her spiritual activities, he did not interfere with this part of her life. He was a good and loving father to Jeffery and provided the discipline that he needed. Theirs was a marriage of convenience and until now it had worked for all. Both she and Ferrell had stable jobs they liked and Jeffery seemed to be quite happy and well adjusted. However, when differences or difficulties arose between them, communication or mutual resolution was impossible. Ferrell withdrew into himself and seemed content to be with his male friends, playing with Jeffery and following his sporting interests.

Although Helen did not know exactly what her future held, she did know that whatever it was, a life of accommodation was not part of it. She needed to be able to embrace her spiritual values and direction from God wholeheartedly and without compromise. If she was this dissatisfied in their marriage, she truly believed that this was true for some part of Ferrell as well. In April, she worked up the courage to tell Ferrell she wanted a divorce. He just listened to her and did not respond in any way. As the days turned into weeks, he avoided her. It was obvious that he had no intention of discussing the subject with her or to face the reality of her unhappiness and intention to divorce him.

Helen allowed Ferrell a few months to himself to consider divorce before trying to speak with him again. But when she was ready to bring it up again, he was about to leave on a business trip to Texas for about six weeks. She decided to await his return to speak with him. Helen was now working as a management analyst on the executive staff at Marshall Space Flight Center and frequently traveled to Washington, DC for training. Shortly after Ferrell returned home from Texas in July, she left for extended training in Washington. As it turned out, they kept missing each other in this way and never got around to discussing divorce again because Ferrell suffered a heart attack in late 1963.

Even though Helen wanted out of the marriage, she loved Ferrell and cared about his health and well-being. So she dropped all notions of divorce and focussed entirely on Ferrell's health. As he recuperated, Helen began to notice that something had changed in him. An energy of kindness radiated from him and he was more gentle and considerate in his feelings and behavior towards her and Jeffery. Helen had always seen this side of him but it had seemed held captive within the stern silence always around him. She was happy for Ferrell because she felt this softening was essential to his complete recovery and she wanted this more than anything else in the world.

A few months after his heart attack, Ferrell wrote Helen a letter telling her how much he loved her. Although she knew he loved her, this was the first time he had told her so directly. Helen was astounded. Although he did not address the possibility of changing himself to keep them together, it was obvious that he wanted that desperately. It was Helen's hope that perhaps the heart attack gave him the necessary physical release to try to work at it. Shortly thereafter, Ferrell regained his strength enough to return to work and they each resumed their regular activities.

For Helen though, there was a very troubling outcome of Ferrell's heart attack. After he recovered, Ferrell made it a point to ask his brother Glenn to take care of Jeffery if anything happened to him. Even allowing for the lingering effects of the recent trauma of facing his mortality, this act hurt her deeply. As she released this pain to God, several questions formed in her mind. Why would he believe her incapable of taking care of Jeffery in his absence and why, with his own negative experience with Glenn, would he trust his son to his brother? She knew that his request came out of a deep love and concern for Jeffery's well-being and that it was not intended to hurt her. This was not something she felt comfortable discussing with Ferrell. Even with his change of behavior towards her, he still had problems talking to her and still did not feel a need to give his reasons for anything.

Helen prayed for help and guidance. Her prayers led her to the troubling possibility that somewhere within himself Ferrell knew he was going to die. From that internal perspective, she felt he questioned whether it was within Helen's destiny to be able to care for Jeffery. Both of these possibilities pained her. Even though she wanted to be free from their relationship, she did not want Ferrell to die and she could not imagine life without Jeffery. These possibilities were more than she could cope with at the time and she placed them in God's hands to work out what was best for all.

At the time, Helen's professional career was really taking off at Marshall. She had demonstrated an exceptional aptitude for administration as executive secretary to Mr. Maus. With his unconditional confidence, she managed much of the day-to-day activity of his Central Planning Office. Helen spoke of him with great warmth and appreciation. He believed in and trusted her abilities and somehow knew just how to support their development. During their long working relationship he often relied on her analytical mind, political savvy and sound judgment to get things done without his direct involvement. He was the one who encouraged her to take the management analyst position because of the career limitations of an executive secretary. Even though she no longer worked directly for him as an analyst, she still worked as a part of the executive staff, of which he was the director. To be eligible for the analyst job, she successfully passed an assortment of examinations that helped to bolster her growing self-confidence. She seemed to flourish in this role and her skills were highly regarded.

As life returned to normal in the Parrish household, Helen began taking flying lessons. Later that year she soloed and received her private pilot's license. This was part of her self-imposed process of expanding her horizons. She said she had to prove to herself that she could master her own fears and learn to accomplish things for which she felt no natural aptitude. Until now, she had done this within her immediate work or home environment, and had done nothing that was at all dangerous. In learning to fly, physically Helen took a giant step towards placing her life in God's hands. As it turned out the risk was well worth it because she loved flying and many barriers in her consciousness broke in different ways to allow her new levels of perspective about life.

In 1964, Helen bought a secondhand airplane of her own. While she was preparing to pick it up in Panama City, Florida, Ferrell had another heart attack. This time his condition was much more serious. She was quite concerned and made the decision in mid-August to take a leave of absence from her job, enabling her to care for Ferrell and to spend more time with him and Jeffery.

Helen had a very loving and caring nature that she expressed without reservation. She had a way of taking this into the smallest details regarding others in her life. Often, she responded to the needs of others long before they knew themselves that they needed something from her. Sometimes, individuals who had trouble ever acknowledging their real need for her love or care, found this quality of her love irritating or offensive. This was the case with Ferrell before his first heart attack. However, this second one made him quite receptive to her love and care during his convalescence over the next several months.

In late November of that year, Helen abruptly awoke from a dream. In the dream, Ferrell came over to her, kissed her and said "Honey, I love you but I just can't go on any longer and I only have six months to live." She knew this was not a dream but rather an inner experience with him. However, nothing seemed to happen and by early 1965 Ferrell's condition had improved to the point where they both returned to their jobs. She had prayed long and hard for his complete healing and was grateful to God for Ferrell's progress to date.

Ever since going back to work after his previous heart attack, Ferrell had frequently missed work because of what he called indigestion. Helen was concerned that this was more than indigestion and repeatedly tried to get him to go to the doctor about it. He was a strong man whose self-image did not allow for the physical weakness he was experiencing. Also, he had a mind of his own

47

and did not like being told to do anything. Even so, Helen could feel his fear concerning his own health. Despite their differences and difficulties, a deep love had grown between them over the years and Helen suffered greatly over Ferrell's declining health.

Then one day in early May, she came home one afternoon from work to find him having another heart attack. He was lying across the bed and complained about suffering from one of his spells of indigestion. Sensing Helen's concern, he assured her that he was not going to work that night and not to worry because this would pass. She was not so sure about that and writes:

"As I watched him, I realized that this was much more severe because it was difficult for him to breathe. He was first pale, then red, in the face and was trying very hard to pretend that he wasn't feeling too bad or that he wasn't worried about himself. I knew that the only way to reach him was to play along. So I casually sat on the edge of the bed and suggested he phone the doctor to get something for his indigestion. He said it would go away in a little while. There was nothing I could do so I left the room to start dinner for Jeffery. I knew he was having a heart attack but somehow I also knew he wasn't going to die right then. However, it was the beginning of the end. Finally about 9:30 p.m. he could no longer rest comfortably on the bed and came into the living room to sit up in a chair. Although Jeffery was already sound asleep in bed, I knew I had to get him to the doctor. By now, his attitude had changed and although he said it wasn't necessary, he was ready for me to call the doctor. How can I ever explain how difficult it was for me calmly to go over to the phone to call, get Jeffery up without causing him alarm and take Ferrell to the hospital?"

Typically this was Helen, monitoring her pain or suffering so as not to let it spill over on anyone else but rather taking it to God for relief. Rarely did she ever talk with strong emotion or panic about how she felt or how difficult something was for her. It always seemed to come out as a matter-of-fact statement. This may be why so many people had difficulty believing that she ever suffered any pain at all, let alone any physical problems of her own.

Within the next three weeks Ferrell had three more heart attacks. After the second attack, Helen phoned their families to suggest that they come down from Medina to see him. The morning after his family arrived he had another one. Helen goes on to write:

"During all this time I prayed. I knew his death was inevitable, I just couldn't let go of him - I refused to let him die. That day as he was having another heart attack, I leaned my head on his bed and silently said a very simple prayer. I told God that I wanted Ferrell to live but if it was his time to die, to take him but please help him to stop struggling and to take him in his sleep. I had to let go of his life because it was now in God's hands."

It was now up to Helen to keep everyone's spirits up. She was able to chat with Ferrell or the family with a smile on her face showing no fear or panic over his condition. Comforting the families was much more difficult than comforting Ferrell. She continues to write:

"From somewhere the strength came - that somewhere was God. The last few years God had been extremely close to me. But now it seemed as if He was walking me around, talking for me, smiling for me, going to work for me and I was just going along because I could do nothing else." Continuing, she writes, "Until now we hadn't spoken of the severity of Ferrell's health or about the number of his heart attacks. The time had come, and was made easy that next afternoon by one of his friends visiting from work. He blundered into the room and said 'When I heard you had three heart attacks, I knew the good Lord was looking out for you.' I turned to the man and said, 'he didn't know,' but Ferrell spoke up and said 'yes, but I knew it was pretty bad though.'"

Shortly after the man left, she had a heart-to-heart-talk with Ferrell. She told him how sick he was and about her prayers after his last attack. Pleading, she asked him to try to relax and stop worrying. He replied that he wasn't worried about himself but about her and Jeffery. In her notes she continues writing:

"I told him God had always taken care of me and always would. Also, I told him not to worry about dying because it was not the end - that you just lose your body and go right on living. For some reason I wasn't able to get into the technicalities of what happens after death. I then left early, hoping to get some rest so that we could continue our talk later."

Helen went home and rather than resting she cleaned the house to ease her worry about Ferrell. Finally she went to bed but at about 10:30 p.m. suddenly she got out of bed feeling the urgent need to go and see Ferrell to finish their talk. She didn't go because she knew it would only upset him. As she settled back in bed, she felt another decline in his condition and asked God to take care of him. While drifting off to sleep in total exhaustion, she saw a vision of Ferrell being buried in the cemetery in Medina. So she was not surprised the next morning when the hospital phoned to tell her that her husband was dead. The date was May 8, 1965.

She writes of her feelings at the time, "I had watched this day approach slowly and painfully and now I felt nothing. I wasn't numb, I wasn't sad, I couldn't cry - I just couldn't feel anything."

Death is never welcome, but at thirty-five with only half a life lived it somehow seems more tragic. Jeffery, who was only six at the time, would never get to know his father or share his life with him. Besides her grief, Helen was in pain because she felt life with her had taken its toll on Ferrell. Where he was content to accept his limitations, Helen was actively working to free herself from hers. This difference in attitude and orientation was huge. It seemed everything

Helen did to gain her freedom left Ferrell feeling threatened and out of control. Apparently he could not go on with Helen, but at the same time he couldn't go back to his old life. Helen always felt that perhaps that deep within himself Ferrell he believed that death was his only escape.

# PART THREE:

# THE PREPARATION

*Frederick R. Kipp*

# Chapter One

Ferrell's body was laid to rest in the family cemetery plot in Medina a few days after his death. As Helen and Jeffery were preparing to return home to Huntsville, Glenn took Helen aside to discuss Jeffery's future. (She knew this was coming but had hoped it could have waited for a few months so that she and Jeffery could make some adjustments in their life without Ferrell.) As Helen tells it:

"Glenn told me that our lives were almost over but we had Jeffery to live for. He wanted Jeffery and me to move into his basement and live with him and his wife. He told me that this was what Ferrell would have wanted for Jeffery and the reason why he asked Glenn to take care of him if anything happened to him."

Now keep in mind that Helen was only thirty-three and Glenn forty-two at the time. She was shocked and saddened that he considered his own life almost over, let alone hers. Glenn was insistent and pleaded with her to consider Jeffery's needs rather than her own. This only added insult to injury. She continues:

"Somehow, and for the time being without offending him, I managed to convince Glenn that my love for Jeffery and our life together in Huntsville were in Jeffery's best interest. However, I knew that this matter was far from over and that Glenn would just find some other way to get what he wanted."

After Ferrell's funeral, life back in Huntsville did not go as smoothly as Helen had hoped. She and Jeffery tried to move on without Ferrell, but as hard as she tried, it seemed as though he really wasn't gone. It had been only a month since his death and she had yet to decide what to do with his personal belongings. For some reason she had resisted going through them as if he might return home from a business trip. Then she began to notice that some of his things were in different places from where she had left them. At first she thought that Jeffery might have moved them and really didn't attach any significance to these occurrences. But as chairs began to move by themselves when she and Jeffery were in the room, it was clear that this was something she could no longer ignore. So finally she accepted that a part of Ferrell's inner being was still living in the house with them.

As she began to acknowledge him, he tried to speak with her. But his disembodied mental faculties were not strong enough to communicate telepathically with Helen. Nevertheless, it was clear that Ferrell did not know he was dead. When she told him, he refused to believe it and continued to hang around. From her previous experience with other deceased beings, she was familiar with this kind of paranormal occurrence, so it didn't frighten her. Even though she understood what was happening, she still wanted him to leave. She asked for the Angelic Messengers of the Christ to escort him to where he needed to be and to explain to him that he was dead and needed to move on. Either he didn't get the message or wasn't ready to go just yet, because he didn't leave.

In time, Ferrell found a way to communicate telepathically with Helen. During this period, Helen said that they actually spent more time interacting than they did when he was alive. He wanted to talk about anything and everything and Helen was shocked by his honest, open and direct manner. This was the first time he had shown any interest in talking to her at any real depth. As appealing as this was, eventually she realized that Ferrell actually liked his disembodied relationship with her and didn't intend to leave anytime soon. This went on for months and she was desperate to move on with her own life.

Finally in early 1966 she took steps to get Ferrell to leave. First, in her mind she created a steel ring around her to keep her feelings contained within it. Daily, through meditation and visualization, she strengthened this ring until it was impenetrable. This prevented him from psychically feeding off her emotional nature and protected her from picking up on his feelings. This was essential because in her previous experiences with the dead, she had been invaded by the strength of their strong psychic feelings of agony or remorse. The emotional channel necessary to communicate at that level drained her and she resolved never to open it up again, not even for Ferrell.

Next, she disposed of all of his personal possessions so that there was nothing of him left in the house. These actions were successful and eventually he left. However, after several days of feeling relief, she also felt a sense of grief by his absence. She said that even though his presence in the house was heavy on her and had pulled her spirits down, she missed it after he was gone. Ferrell returned twice more before leaving for good. The first time was in early April, but there was a difference about him in that he was no longer pulling on her for anything. He was more like a dear friend on whom she could lean, if necessary. The last visit was a few weeks later. She writes about this incident in this way:

"Shortly after lying down to relax one day, a long corridor opened up before me. Then two doors slid open and in the far end of a sloping room was a long and wide concrete box. As I watched the box, the top door opened and Ferrell sat up and looked at me. His eyes were so dark and flashing that they looked almost a dazzling black. There was a rush of love extended to me, authentic but impersonal. In a very kind voice he said 'I don't care what you do.' At that moment I was free of all marital ties to him but left with a love and compassion that was sustaining. When this experience ended and he left, my feelings of aloneness were gone and I once again felt whole. I rarely felt him in the house after that but when I did, it was as if a friend had dropped by to see how I was doing."

Although Helen and Glenn had come to some accommodation about Jeffery, Glenn's behavior did not change. To give Jeffery a sense of being a part of his father's family, and in part to appease Glenn, she and Jeffery began visiting Medina together at least once a year. In addition to this, Jeffery usually spent a few weeks each summer with Glenn and his wife. Although this arrangement seemed to suit both Jeffery and Glenn, it sometimes worked against Helen and her relationship with her son. As each year went by, she wanted to believe that Glenn had accepted the present arrangement, but in actuality, his opposition to it had just gone underground. There were many situations in which he revealed to her, through his subtle and undermining activities, that he still intended to get Jeffery away from her.

In 1968, she was forced to accept that Glenn would go to any length to get Jeffery away from her. One day, a man who claimed to be from the Social Security Administration came to visit her. He asked her strange questions about her personal finances and about her bank account. Then he questioned her about what she did with Ferrell's social security benefit checks. He very authoritatively instructed her that this money was supposed to be saved for Jeffery.

Later she found out that there were no such social security requirements. The surviving parent had the right to use benefits for anything necessary for the child's care. It was then that Helen began to suspect the man was a friend of Glenn's who had agreed to check up on her. She assumed this was an attempt to pressure her to save Ferrell's social security money for Jeffery. Although she later became certain he was Glenn's friend, she thought it might be possible that he actually worked for the Social Security Administration. So she decided not to file a formal complaint against the man which might have led to more problems with Glenn.

Helen was always a strong and loving parent to Jeffery. As a single working mother, she sacrificed and devoted much of herself and her energy for him. During Jeffery's visits to Medina, Glenn and his wife apparently twisted many of the things Jeffery told them about his life with Helen. It was personally difficult and painful for Helen to remain silent when Glenn used these visits to make his case against her to Jeffery. But she refused to defend herself to her son. As the years passed, Helen did her best not to allow the growing gulf of mistrust between her and her brother-in-law to affect Jeffery's relationship with him. As always, she took that pain to God rather than allowing it to build a barrier between her and Jeffery.

In trying to find ways of being understanding of Glenn's behavior, she said she later realized that Jeffery's presence had seemed to enliven Glenn, to the extent that it gave him a reason to go on living. His statement at the funeral "Our life is almost over but we have Jeffery to live for" now made more sense to her.

She always felt that Glenn was truly sorry about the way he treated her but he honestly believed that his behavior and actions were necessary for him to fulfill the trust Ferrell placed in him before he died.

As Helen worked to rebuild her life, she discovered that Ferrell's death affected her more deeply than just the personal loss. In many ways it seemed as though it represented a greater death of her former life and conditioning in Tennessee. Even though she had done much to requalify and change herself, as long as Ferrell was in her life she had accommodated aspects of her past to please Ferrell. His death was a catalyst which propelled her forward to focus on her own priorities and direction. Through God's guidance, a new pattern of spiritual work emerged within her that continued for years. She began her new life through what she referred to as a death and rebirthing cycle. This was a new foundation upon which her later life and work would be built. This also served as the pivotal focus for the next level of regeneration work on her body.

In the wake of Ferrell's death, Helen seriously looked at her life and identified the patterns of routine activity. She felt how restrictive they had become to the freedom she desired in her life. She had mistakenly believed that life away from rural Tennessee would be more exciting. Although she found the move to be beneficial, she was quite disappointed when her general assumptions about life proved to be wrong.

Creative change and movement had become the keynote of her life, because without it, as she said, "Life is just plain boring." At work, as she watched the people around her in the office, she realized that everyone had routines that made their lives bearable and worth living. She previously thought that automatic routine was peculiar only to farm life. But now she had to face that it was not particular to any social strata or location, but rather it was a major factor of all human life. She noticed that although people complained about being caught in the grind of their life, they really wanted and needed the security that the routine provided and did little or nothing to change it. It seemed as though most of the people she knew were going to live and die in their unconscious patterns of daily life. This was not a pleasant realization, nor was it something she wanted for herself.

Helen found that she had to come to terms with the fact that there was nothing mainstream about her life or values. Although she was perfectly able to function in the outer world amongst people, she was not interested in the outer activities or recreation that most people were drawn toward and centered their lives around. She needed to be consistently challenged and stimulated to maintain the focus and momentum of her work. There came a point where her relationship with God was the only activity which truly sustained her. She didn't grow bored with God because, as she grew internally, her connection with God was continually changing as well. She wrote:

"He was always one step ahead of me and if I wasn't careful, He could be a million steps ahead before I knew what happened - finding that out was exciting to me. God was the one thing in my life I could not beat!"

Helen continued her study of philosophy, psychology, metaphysics, and the sciences. In science she was particularly interested in physics and the relationship between energy and matter. She was drawn to the idea of relating "Energy" to what she referred to as "Spirit." Intuitively she recognized a potent connection between religion and the other disciplines she was studying. From different perspectives and using different methods, she saw that they were all basically trying to understand the nature and essence of God. However, because religion was the only discipline openly claiming that purpose, it had become the preeminent authority on the subject.

Helen came upon a series of letters to the editor of *The News York Times* written in the 1930s by the author and philosopher, Walter Russell, and several well-known scientists. These were about the forces in nature and their philosophical and scientific role in cosmology. It wasn't until she read these that she began to consciously accept and relate to God as "The Energy" underlying all space, time and matter. This was an exciting revelation for her. In her feeling nature, Helen had a lifetime of experiences that documented God as energy. This was the basis of her physical rituals, her experience on the inner realms of life, her trust in her active intuition and so on. Before now, she had never connected consciously the unseen realm of energy to the "energy" as defined by science. This gave her life experience new internal meaning and structure, as well as relevance in the external world.

She did not consider this shift in perspective as heretical, but rather the beginning of a more cohesive and comprehensive extension of her knowledge of God. This new internal development confirmed to her that she was moving in the right direction. The fact that there was no external proof to support God as energy or that conventional religious belief rejected this radical notion, did not dissuade her from her quest to know more.

# Chapter Two

There was another aftermath of Ferrell's death that hit Helen hard. The reality and strength of the human conditioning towards death was now much more apparent to her. It was no longer some remote possibility in the distant future but a glaring physical reality which she now had to face directly in her life. She felt a new immediacy and an internal driving force to go after her own physical and psychological conditioning of accepting death as inevitable. A book she was reading at the time proved helpful with this task. It described in detail how consciousness works by giving examples through various individuals with their own psychological complexes. This was intriguing to Helen since she was especially drawn to unraveling all aspects within herself which limited her conscious awareness in any way. With the tools and guidelines from the book, along with her trust in God, Helen embarked on a journey to examine the roots of her own psyche. Fully committed, she began looking at her reactions and responses to every single person, situation and event in her life.

At first, this seemed overwhelming and impossible. But she prayed to God to show her just how she was conditioned by her environment and her every experience in life. As she continued this disciplined focus, she found herself entering into a dimension of darkness. With the visualizations the Holy Spirit gave her, she felt as if she were at the bottom of a barrel. Every time she closed her eyes to look at her life, she found herself in a dark cave with no light to show her the way out. She felt trapped by her own unconsciousness. In facing this dilemma, she knew she could not return to the life she had left behind. There was no choice but to continue forward and once again consciously surrender herself more deeply to God. This began a four-year period of intense introspection and transmutation. About this time period she said:

"I knew that one day I would see some light again. When I felt a limitation, rather than reacting, I was shown how to look at it and to think about how it got there in the first place. Then I was shown how to devise a way to crack it loose so it could be removed. I found out that when it cracked, the psychological shattering within me would make me feel like I was going insane. However, I knew that if I could hold on to God's guiding energy for all I was worth, that this feeling would pass and I would feel balance return to my consciousness."

During this cycle, her free time was very limited. She was loaded down by her various roles and responsibilities in the outer world as well as being a mother. The difficulty of scheduling time to handle any one of them satisfactorily was justification enough for her to consider quitting her commitment to self-analysis.

However, in spite of the difficulties and challenges, she stuck with it. After this prolonged period of intensely demanding work, the day finally came when she closed her eyes and saw herself walking out of the cave into light all around her.

This "God-led descent" into the dark realm of Helen's unconscious life and out again into the light was symbolic of the mythical path to selfhood. Through this process, Helen reclaimed the parts of her feminine expression held captive in unconsciousness because they did not conform to the conventional female image in the outer world and in collective consciousness. This was her psycho-spiritual journey of integration of the more assertive feminine qualities of her being into her conscious life. While in her cave of darkness, the naive and impressionable young woman that she was died. Through the Light of her God Self, she was lifted to a new level of inner balance, self-authority and outer independence. Although the next inner psychological foundation for freedom was now in place, actual freedom of expression would come only by openly living it as a reality in the world.

This is an exceptionally difficult and challenging task for anyone to undertake. (Men have a similar journey specific to the male conditioning.) For women, the externalization process often brands them as aggressive, conniving and arrogant. This has the tendency to incite both men and women alike to put "the offender" in her place. From that day forward, she said the process and path that God revealed to her, and she had followed, automatically took over in her life. She said:

"No longer did I have to work as hard at changing my consciousness or fret from day to day about finding the next unconscious pattern to change because I had a deeper conviction and knowing that God would reveal it to me. Every time I ran across a restriction in the way I thought, felt or acted, I would say to myself, 'Well okay if that is the way you are, you are going to be bound by it unless you change it.'"

Most all the actions she took during this period were personal to her and didn't involve other people. She found that some of the hardest limitations to change in herself were those social and cultural norms imprinted in her through childhood. The cultural morality of her early conditioning was so interwoven within recorded energy of her life and body, that they effectively blocked change. Sometimes she even got physically ill when considering a challenge to these deeply seated mores. She encountered this kind of collective psychological intimidation each time she began to seriously challenge one of these constraints. In the process, she also found that when she risked all by changing her behavior, each small victory weakened the cumulative hold of the subconscious. To her, this was a surprising gift from God and became the key to her remarkable ability to live according to her spiritual guidance fully and practically at increasing degrees in her life.

Helen continued her practice of observing people as a pastime to help make conscious and internalize the vast array of human behavior. By watching co-workers in her office, she realized that the way she had been taught to live her life was not the only way or the best way for everyone. She felt it was important to continue making this distinction in allowing others their freedom to be. She liked and admired many who had very different values and lifestyles than her own. Over a period of about a year, she began to more fully understand and appreciate the differences of each person's individual path and how it seemed to perfectly suit them. Through her own analytical process, she questioned that if life was so full of different moral and social values and others seem to live theirs so easily, why then did she feel so limited by the ones she was taught?

She concluded that just because these patterns had been anchored there by someone or something else, they were not inherently right or true for her. The only way for her to get free of this early programming was to either consciously verify their truth and claim them for herself, or to challenge them and change herself and her behavior. She further realized that what she knew as truth at any given time might be only a temporary step towards knowing the next truth and more of God in the process. In essence, truth is not locked in time and evolves with every expansion in consciousness.

Helen's first experience in breaking the limitation of morally appropriate feminine behavior was to have an affair. This was a huge and drastic step for her! She really had no interest or desire for an affair but chose it to start with because it was so contrary to her very being. Therefore, she thought she would get the most out of the experience. Once she made up her mind to follow it through, she carefully considered each man in her office as a possibility. She settled on someone whom she considered a "man of the world" and who was known in the office for having had many affairs. She thought him not only suitable but also harmless and therefore an unlikely threat to her. Another plus was that he had a seemingly liberated personality which made her feel free to approach him honestly and directly.

One afternoon she found the courage to sit down at his desk to tell him that she wanted to have an affair with him. She stated that it would be short in duration and that she wanted it understood that she was free to break it off at any time. When she was finished speaking, his face turned absolutely white as he mumbled "Well, I...I...,I Okay...I think...yes." Before she could change her mind, they arranged a time and a place to meet and she left his office.

She had no idea what she was getting herself into or what was about to happen. Helen had a very clinical way of describing very emotionally charged situations in her life. This came from the fact that with any given situation, when she was shattered by the experience, she went into the depth of pain or agony over it and came out with considerable self-knowledge, understanding and power over that part of her life. So, in speaking about the day that they finally met for the affair, she simply stated "We met at the arranged place and time and had sex one time." Of course it was not that simple and the result on Helen was devastating.

For three days she lay in bed with a high fever. During this time she lost twenty pounds as she dealt with everything in her that had been challenged or hit by her behavior. (This may sound difficult to believe, but the strength of Helen's relationship with God and "Energy" was such that her bodily experiences often defied logic.) Her personality felt shattered into pieces. Within herself, as well as all around her, she could hear the voices of her parents, their ministers and others condemning her. Just to survive those three days the only thing she could do was to trust in God's care.

Several days after returning to work, the man waited for her in the hall as she reported to work. He told her not to worry because a lot of people have affairs, that there is nothing to be upset about and that she shouldn't feel ashamed. Very directly she told him that what he said had nothing to do with what she was feeling or experiencing. Not giving away just how fragile she remained over the incident, she calmly explained that she was breaking a barrier in consciousness and would get through it just fine, thank you. Although her comments obviously upset him, he did not say anything more at the time.

Apparently, Helen and this man were both part of a work-related consciousness-raising group that met regularly to chat and explore the various theories and techniques popular at the time. During one of these meetings while he and Helen were talking, he told her that the way to control people was the same way that you control animals - when you find out what they need, you give it to them, but only after you get them to do what you want first. The implicit message in this statement, that he intended to get control of her, was not missed by Helen. As she sat across from him, she said she let a smile come to her mouth and silently she thought, "You son of a bitch, I've got news for you, buddy. If you think you can get control of me, you are sadly mistaken!"

The next day at work she phoned him to tell him that she had experienced and learned what she needed and that it was all over between them. Again, he seemed dumbfounded by her directness and with a hurt sound in his voice said, "Why did you have to call to tell me, couldn't you just let it end naturally?" Perhaps that was the indirect way others acted in these situations, but Helen was learning about the freedom of being consciously direct - and after all, she was only doing what they had agreed to at the beginning.

In this incident, Helen's courage and commitment to change along with her willingness to risk, began a more active externalization phase which served as the foundation for the identity she was creating. She had stepped out and apart from the accepted norms of female behavior of the time to claim for herself the inherent right of independent action. Not only had she initiated the series of events, she had also ended them. More importantly for her, through this man's treatment of her, she had directly and squarely faced the collective masculine agreement against such female behavior. Even in her state of emotional devastation, she felt good about herself and what she had accomplished. Although this did not feel like a major victory for her at the time, nevertheless it was and it launched her into a series of similar external experiences and victories.

She had started with an affair, the worst possible personal situation she could imagine, and then had proceeded to identify other aspects of her conditioning that were limitations to her expression of freedom in the world. In the same gutsy and direct fashion, she knocked them off one at a time. At this point in her life, her only goal was to keep expanding her consciousness in order to increase her freedom to be and to live without the restrictions of matter. As with her other numerous activities, in time it became easier for her to trust God to show her what to do next to disassemble the unconscious patterns and structures of limitation within her. This was always followed by the Christ reassembling the pieces of her life to give her even greater freedom of expression. God's guidance, through the Holy Spirit and Its transformative power through the Christ, increasingly was the sole sustaining energy source of her life. Once embarking down this path and experiencing the true sense of freedom available, there was no turning back to the life she had once lived.

# Chapter Three

By the end of 1965, Helen had made many significant personal changes within herself as she more deeply explored and expanded her relationship with God and the Ascended Masters. However, still she did not feel the sense of purpose or direction she needed. Without this clarity of spiritual purpose, she felt bound by the form of her life. This abruptly changed on December 13, 1965, the day she said, "Her new life in Spirit began." It was a Monday and she had risen early so she could make a regular work prayer group meeting at 7:00 a.m. She writes:

"I wasn't overjoyed at attending the meeting because although the group had much dedication to God and talked a lot about what that meant, they really couldn't get down to the basics of deep felt prayer - and I didn't feel moved to try to assist in any way. Like everything else in my life, I was there but not a part of it - totally alone. As the meeting closed, each person asked the group to pray for someone. When it got to me, I asked them to pray for me. I said that God answers my prayers so profoundly that I'm almost afraid to pray. So, I need your help to get past the fear that the answer will forever change my life. Further, I told them, I want to find a reason for living - not that I'm going to commit suicide or anything. A dear man spoke up and restated my request as 'You want to know God's purpose for you' and I replied, that's it."

"I left the meeting and went to the office to begin work. On the way up in the elevator I said God, you have to help me. I am always so tired and I don't know what to do! When I sat down at my desk, something struck me in the head - I don't mean an object, but rather a feeling - and for a minute, I thought I would fall out of my chair. Although this had happened a few times in the past few weeks, this time I knew it happened as a direct result of my plea for God's help. This is a bit difficult to explain, but suddenly I didn't feel so low of spirit anymore and I really couldn't remember why I had felt so low in the first place.

As I thought about what had happened, my mind went to the man who had summed up my prayer request and I decided he was praying for me. He later confirmed that he had indeed been praying for me when this all happened. For the balance of the day I felt pressure building up inside me to do something. So, later that afternoon after returning home from work, I laid down on the couch to rest and pray. The pressure got so bad that I even asked Jesus for help."

"I prayed for each person in our prayer group, some others that came to mind and of course for myself. In my prayers, I told God and the Ascended Masters that I had done all I could do, that something must happen because I couldn't go on with my life as it was. I saw myself separate from my body, go up through my own Higher Self towards Jesus, then past him to sit on my stool beside God. God told me that my life was one of None-Expression. To help me understand, I was asked to look at the grass on earth. It didn't try to become trees or flowers, and the flowers didn't try to become trees or grass. Then it was explained to me that the human kingdom was spending all its time trying to externally copy each other and not enough time trying to be and accept what and who they were, internally. My job was to assist others to find and appreciate, within themselves, their individual uniqueness and true beauty. I was to do this without telling them what to believe or what to do."

"Naturally I was overjoyed that God talked to me about my purpose in life. For so long now I've walked down a drab hallway with too much knowledge and without being able to stop myself from getting more. Now, I walk in this hallway with a golden glow of understanding of the reason for the knowledge I've been given and appreciation for what I will continue to receive. My life changed forever with this experience, but by the next morning I began to wonder what it meant and how to do it."

During the next year Helen worked to integrate this inner experience and knowledge into the various dimensions of her daily life. She continued to expose herself to new ways of thinking and feeling about her connection with God and the Universe. As she turned thirty-four in 1966, she said she felt reborn into a life of God's design.

Sometime during late 1965 or early 1966, Helen met the spiritual leaders of an organization in Colorado. It was a spiritual growth activity, whose major focus was on the Ascended Masters. There were several things that attracted Helen to this group. The most important was that they taught people how to contact and truly know their "I AM Presence" or Individual God Self. The purpose of this was to learn how to call on or activate their internal connection through the power of God to transform their life. This is the Divine Connection within each individual person through which the energy of God flows to the totality of their being.

Coming across this group was a monumental event in Helen's life. This "I AM Presence" was the internal God connection that she had always known within herself but could never name. She now had access to fellowship with others who knew the guidance, beauty, love and power of this Divine Spark of Light within. In addition, she was introduced to an incredible assortment of books and written material defining and describing the reality and nature of this Presence. This included information on the energy connection between the God Self and the Universe, down through the unseen cosmic planes of energy life to the manifested Earth. She learned that this connection was made through a series of unseen or subtle energy levels called planes. In addition to planes, there are other levels of human energy bodies that are interconnected to each other, the physical body and the Earth. This perspective of planes and subtle bodies helped to open deeper intuitive channels within Helen for greater self-awareness and understanding of the inner dimensions of life.

This gold mine of resources also included a direct connection to the Christ energy work being carried on by Hierarchies of Ascended Masters, Archangels and other Cosmic Beings. This connection came through the group leaders in the form of dictations. (Dictations are a type of channeling whereby a trained individual receives direct communication from an Ascended Master or other inner Being, usually spoken in a group setting.)

The membership also believed in physical body perfection, or ascension. This is possible when the God Self is given enough access and freedom to transform and raise the matter of the physical body, through a Christed alignment and consciousness, so that it does not have to go through the process of death. Rather than dying (at a normal point of death) the physical body will advance and pass directly, with its consciousness, to the next level or higher form of life, while at the same time dematerializing the physical body.

Helen began to see, then later accept, physical body ascension as the collective Divine Plan for all people on Earth and as the goal of human and planetary evolution. For those who are willing to become conscious of their own Divine Presence and to receive and follow the guidance of the Christ Energy, there is the opportunity to get free from the evolutionary path and cycle of reembodiment. By surrendering to the Christ Energy, an individual enters an accelerated or initiatory path towards physical ascension.

This was most definitely Helen's path and purpose in life. She was grateful to God for leading her to this group with their perspectives, resources and support. A spiritual road map was beginning to unfold before her and she felt revitalized by how God was directing her.

# Chapter Four

In 1966, Helen's life accelerated and became even more hectic. In addition to her responsibilities as a single mother, her work and regular prayer, meditation and study regimen, she was now traveling to Colorado for classes and training to become a group leader in this organization. Although she did her best not to let all this activity adversely affect Jeffery, there was no way to avoid it. Physically, she was stretched so thin that she barely had enough energy just to get through the week, let alone for the weekend group work and travel. She was caught between two potent forces in her life - her love and devotion to Jeffery, and her love and devotion to God as her purpose for living. This kind of dilemma is painful and difficult enough for any parent, but especially so for a mother.

As 1966 progressed into 1967, her life and schedule became even more complex. Helen began dating a man she met whom she liked and with whom she felt personally and spiritually compatible. She decided to move slowly and cautiously and in time their relationship deepened. So, when this man made the decision to take a job in Detroit, this brought about a crisis in both of their lives. What would happen to their relationship with this move? On his part, he resolved his crisis by asking Helen to marry him. She was confronted with another test of her commitment to follow her own dedication to purpose.

This threw Helen into a dilemma because from a practical viewpoint, marriage would solve some very pressing problems for her and Jeffery. Although she was a loving and caring mother to Jeffery, she was deeply concerned that without a father to share masculine viewpoints and values, his life would not be balanced or complete. However, she was just not ready to jump into another marriage so soon after Ferrell's death. At all costs she wanted to avoid an impulsive or emotionally charged decision. So, as he made his move to Detroit, it was decided that Helen would visit him as much as possible and that they would discuss marriage at a later time.

Helen focused her attention on the prospect of marriage. She knew she needed a partner, not only to help with raising Jeffery, but also to share her unique spiritual orientation as well as her commitment to the rigors of continuous self-analysis and personal growth. From her experience with this man, it seemed possible, if not likely, that he was a match. After a few visits to Detroit, however, it was painfully clear that her assessment was wrong. He was indeed a kind and loving man with many endearing qualities, but he was also a product of his generation which included masculine control and domination of any relationship with a woman.

All of her human conditioning compelled her to want to ignore these facts and to marry him anyway. It was as if a crowd of people had invaded her mind and body to tell her what she should and must do for Jeffery's sake and for her future security as a woman. As difficult as the internal struggle was over this situation, God had prepared her well to cut through the mental and emotional miasma to face the realities of the situation. Her only path to freedom was to proceed without encumbrance. Realizing this, she withdrew from the relationship and moved forward alone. This was a severe blow to Helen. It triggered the next level of crisis by breaking more of her life conditioning in her body and consciousness.

Helen's involvement in the encounter and Transactional Analysis groups continued and grew in intensity. Apparently her sincere and earnest dedication to spiritual growth was so visible and compelling to others in these groups that she began to attract attention. A few of the more serious members began to seek her out to talk about their own experiences with their work on themselves. She in turn began to share with them some of the principles of Light and Energy that she was learning and teaching in Colorado. By the end of 1967, more people were attracted to this group, and they were by then frequent visitors to Helen and Jeffery's home.

One ritual she shared that seemed to be of greatest interest was that of "decreeing." Decreeing is a deliberate individual or group activity, using repetitively spoken words or phrases, to invoke and anchor higher creative energies for the purpose of change and transmutation. The components of decreeing have been around for centuries in the form of mantras, chants, affirmations, invocations and hymns.

Helen used decrees to break down and transmute her barriers in consciousness. As a result, the Holy Spirit taught her how to use visualization to become a conscious participant in the process of change. Through decrees, she strengthened her spiritual will to better align and synchronize her thoughts, feelings and actions to support the changes taking place in her life. Using clairvoyance, she learned how to see and stand witness to the reality and power of God's descending Energies invoked as they worked through all the activities of her life.

By late 1967, Helen's travel schedule for training and group meetings had progressed to the point where she requested a government transfer from Huntsville to a government facility in Colorado. But to her disappointment, there were no openings. At the time this was a blow because it would have saved her a lot of stress and would have made it unnecessary to leave Jeffery with someone else when she made her frequent trips. However, it turned out to be a blessing that the transfer did not come through.

As Helen spent more and more time with this group, she became increasingly troubled by what she experienced. This mainly related to the position of "Messenger for the Ascended Masters" held by one of the spiritual leaders. She was uncomfortable with much of the content of his dictations. It seemed to her that rather than being spiritually challenging and enlightening, his dictations became more self-serving and authoritative. They were executed in a way that set the stage for him to exert control over his students. This bothered Helen deeply. She was actively working to break her own restrictions in consciousness and here was this teacher trying to create new ones. Internally, she knew this was not the kind of teacher God was leading her to be.

Also, Helen was concerned about the way group decrees were being directed personally against those individuals and institutions that opposed the group's purpose, perspectives, and activities. Neither of the leaders was accustomed to any form of challenge to their teaching methods, so you can imagine that they were less than happy when Helen began to gently speak her mind about things. Intuitively she knew that it was just a matter of time before she left this organization and she was again desperate for new direction from God.

The opening for this guidance came in 1968 during a spiritual conference in Denver. Attending were two women from Los Angeles, representing a group called the I AM Reading Room. The leader of this group, Esther, had been reaching out to other I AM Presence groups for new energy and vitality for her organization. This is how Esther had met the other group leaders. While they were working out of their Los Angeles location, from time to time they gave classes, conducted services, or gave dictations at the I AM Reading Room headquarters.

Esther was a remarkable woman who had a very solid and intimate relationship with the Ascended Masters. Through her contact and receptivity to them, she had learned about the principle of transmutation (generally referring to the raising and purification of one's lower nature and matter through the Christ Consciousness) and had received a number of practical and potent lessons, rituals and tools. In conversations at various conferences, Esther spoke to Helen about the various techniques she was teaching in Los Angeles. There were two in particular that caught Helen's attention. The first was something called "chart work" used for personal transmutation and the conscious direction of energy for creative manifestation. The second was what Esther called "clearance work" (a clairvoyant clearing technique). A basic explanation of each might give some context for how these activities fit into Helen's life and why she considered them so important in her work.

Throughout Helen's adult life, she was involved in various self-development groups as well as Transactional Analysis and the Colorado spiritual activity. None of these were sufficient in and of themselves for the work to which Helen was being led. However, each contributed certain essential principles and techniques that she embraced and practiced in her life. She noticed in her personal transmutation work, that leading up to breaking each particular restriction to higher consciousness, her vital energy level became so low that she was barely able to get through the day. Furthermore, she noticed that if she persevered in her stand, shortly thereafter not only did her energy return but it was much higher than before. So, when she was introduced to the principle of transmutation she began to understand the importance and reason for what she had experienced.

As Divine Beings in the image of God, we enter our dense physical plane existence with access to the energy contained within our own Higher Self. We also enter the energy field contained within the Earth environment as our new home. It is through the interaction and relationship of our individualized stream of God's energy with that of the Earth domain, that we learn to become what Helen called "co-creators" with God. It is within this co-creator process that we meet our purpose in God and reclaim our Divine essence and identity.

As Energy Beings taking physical form, we descend down through the various invisible spiritual planes of existence towards physical plane life. Throughout this descent and eventual physical incarnation, we are always connected to an abundant source of limitless energy in God. However, over the eons of evolutionary time that it took to prepare and condition the human body to receive our Spirit, the dense or lower vibration of matter of this earth plane deadened our sensory awareness of our original energy source in God. Then gradually, out of necessity for survival, our creative nature became focused on learning how to transform the matter of our new earth environment into an energy form which would sustain our physical life and bodies in the world. This was our part in the process of bringing spiritual consciousness into dense matter in God's Creative Plan on Earth.

As we lost conscious connection with our God Self and Its connection to a limitless energy resource to sustain us, we became unconscious creators in a closed system of limitation in matter. As individual beings in this state, we find ourselves in the same condition as the collective human race on the planet today. Increasingly, we are using up available and nonrenewable physical energy resources from the earlier creative cycles, crystallized in matter. Therefore, our inherent and dwindling energy supply is locked up within our personal and collective unconscious creations. We have learned ways to unlock, use and deplete that crystallized energy in the matter of the earth and our bodies, with no real understanding of how to draw and use our true spiritual source energy in God to sustain our life when the other is gone.

Helen felt that, throughout time, the purpose of every religion and spiritual movement, and more recently science and psychology, is to refocus our conscious attention back towards the unlimited source of energy beyond our known universe. To make this reconnection, we must unlock and reclaim the crystallized energy captured within the form of our lives. It is this reclaimed or transmuted energy that enables us to reorient our consciousness from a material orientation towards a spiritual one. This new spiritual orientation acknowledges and embraces God's unlimited love and energy not only as the source of our life, but also the source of all that we know as the visible world and universe around us. Helen's ongoing commitment to transmutation became her path toward becoming a conscious co-creator with God.

Before her contact with Esther, Helen had adapted certain psychological, metaphysical, and transformational techniques to work on her commitment to consciousness. As Esther spoke about her "chart work," Helen saw how practical and valuable this new energy tool could be. Chart work consists of a twelve-sectioned circle in which an individual symbolically stands in the center. Each section represents a negative quality to be changed or transmuted into its corresponding positive or divine quality. Also included in each section is a quality of God's energy given to accomplish the transformation as well as the Ascended Master, Angelic Host and Divine Hierarchy working with that particular quality of Light. In essence, this is a way of learning to work and receive the various aspects of the transforming Christ energy within ourselves and the world around us.

When Esther described what she called "clearance work," Helen was enthralled by its potential application in her life and work. Immediately she saw clearance work as a form of prayer, but one in which the participant is actively involved and informed throughout the process. In brief, clearance usually involves people working together using clairvoyant faculties. Each must be thoroughly trained and prepared for the use of God's "higher" and more potent creative energies. The process works by one person, the seer, "looking in" on the inner planes clairvoyantly, identifying the ethereal limitations, restrictions, blocks and locks that disrupt inner balance and alignment. These problems, at the level of our inner bodies, usually manifest in our outer life as personality patterns or complexes resulting in conflict, struggle, pain and disease.

The second person's role is one of directing energy by making "calls" or asking God's energies to clear what is seen from the inner bodies. As this happens, the seer clairvoyantly watches the energy do Its work. The time it takes to do the clearance work and for it to take effect depends on the experience of the clearance team and the knowing faith and diligence of the person receiving the work.

As with all prayer activity, energy works from the inside out and requires that individuals be receptive to God revealing to them the root cause or source of the problem within themselves. Also, they must be willing and committed to take the necessary actions for change in their life to activate their responsibility in the process of clearance resolution. Helen already knew the power of prayer in her life and saw clearance as an extension of it. In using clearance, she understood it was God's energy and authority doing the work but now she had access to the inner plane dimensions for greater information and understanding.

Throughout Helen's life, she had a long history of taking responsibility for herself and intuiting what was happening internally as well as around her in her environment. So when Esther and her partner first did clearance on Helen during a particular conference, immediately she felt and knew the truth and power of the work for herself. The Holy Spirit once again had led her to the right time and place to begin her next level of preparation. At the end of the conference, Esther invited Helen to come to Los Angeles to take classes, receive clearance training and to work with her.

*Frederick R. Kipp*

# PART FOUR:

# THE TEACHER

*Frederick R. Kipp*

# Chapter One

When God calls your number, life is never the same! It was in the fall of 1967 that Helen first began to get an inkling of what her future might become. Since December 1965, more and more people were attracted to her in ways she did not understand. Because she valued her privacy and independence, she did not actively look to attract attention or advise anyone. But somehow, God had brought a kind of radiance to her presence and life that was magnetic. However, she began to notice that no matter how much she wanted to retain her privacy, she still felt compelled to expand her interaction with people far beyond her personal preference and comfort.

Keep in mind that Helen always gave people exactly what she herself needed the most. Spiritually speaking, this meant supporting others to go directly to their own God Self for all the answers they ever needed in life. She thought it odd that people were drawn to her for guidance and direction. This was a new experience for her. For Helen, believing something to be true for herself was one thing, but to teach the principles of that truth to others was an entirely different matter. Even when she verified something for herself, she never asked anyone else to accept it without confirmation for themselves. But if this was God's plan for her, she was open and receptive to the work.

By 1968, Helen's public life began to overtake her cherished world of personal solitude and communion with God. Her travel continued and she interacted with even more people in a life that already left her exhausted. During the year, her association and activity with the Colorado group gradually diminished, but she also began to travel to Los Angeles for training with Esther through the I Am Reading Room. For a period of time she was involved with both organizations and was traveling to both locations.

This was not an easy time. The intensity of Helen's life had reached the point where she was so stressed that she couldn't sleep. It was as if with every personal breakthrough in consciousness she experienced or every plateau of group activity that was reached, God showed her something else to do. She felt as if she was coming apart at the seams. She thought working for God and spiritual growth was supposed to stabilize one's life and make it better, not worse. At one point, things got so bad that while driving home from one of her group sessions in Montgomery, she screamed out loud for God's help because she just didn't think she could go on. As in the past, when God's energy moved on her, she felt it physically. This time she felt a blow to her head, like an ax had hit her, then felt the tension drain from her body. Although she was grateful for the release, Helen realized she needed to find a greater sense of balance with all she was juggling in her life.

Her clairvoyant skills and activities continued to expand and become more integrated and practical in nature. In the beginning, her telepathic conversations with the Masters were always conducted on some high, inner plane. However, with time and practice she began to experience these discussions at lower levels in her consciousness. Her inner and outer realms continued to converge and her experiences began to manifest themselves at the level of her everyday life and within her physical sense perception. One in particular stood out to her.

As she engaged in one of these inner conversations, suddenly the Christ came into her living room and sat in a chair across from her. He told her it was time for her to begin living her purpose in life by reflecting and revealing to people their true and magnificent beauty in the Christ. He added that in this process, she would find a new depth and dimension of her own Christ essence. Before leaving, He promised always to be with her and that He would speak with her often. From this experience Helen finally accepted that her privacy would continue to diminish as God bought more people into her life regardless of her personal feelings. Therefore she prepared herself for this transition in every way that she could.

As she continued her training with Esther, she threw herself into this work with the same intensity and passion that she did in all of her transformational work. Increasingly she felt pressure from her own Higher Self to prepare for whatever the future had in store for her. She became more acquainted with the various Ascended Masters and the seven ray energies made available to the I AM students through chart work. (The Seven Rays represent the diversified activities of cosmic creation energies from God. They are aspects of the spiritual life forces manifesting in seven different ways and seven different phases or activities of development. These rays are directed to the earth through the seven Elohim, Archangels and Chohans.)

Helen not only saw these beings and energies, but also felt their presence in her life. Her orientation towards this inner realm deepened, which not only guided her visible life, but also greatly enriched it. Often the results of this orientation were particularly uncomfortable and painful. This was because it involved taking stands and breaking patterns that upset her family and friends. Many times this led to misunderstandings and the hurt feelings of others. However, she knew that she had to follow the guidance she was given from God, the Christ or the Ascended Masters completely and unconditionally. Learning to face and deal with the reactions of others was part of her training.

Of all the Ascended Masters, Helen was the closest to Morya. By now it had been several years since he had begun teaching her and they were speaking regularly. Through this relationship, Helen's telepathic faculties were extended and strengthened. Even though he was her inner teacher, in a way they also became friends. Helen talked to him about things she could not share with anyone else. She said he never pulled punches with her and spoke directly to her questions and concerns. Sometimes his teaching approach shattered her sense of mental agility, certainty and personal control. This was because he could be particularly honest and direct in his communications. At first, she tried to argue with him or engage him in a debate over what he told her that she needed to look at or do. When this happened, he simply withdrew from her and wouldn't return until she had worked through her resistance to what he had said. He told her that it wasn't his responsibility to teach her but rather her responsibility to allow him the freedom to give to her as needed, and for her to learn no matter how this was done.

Morya rarely told Helen what she wanted to hear but always told her what she needed to know. He did not praise her for the positive changes she made within herself but was always there to prompt and encourage her to go deeper in change. He always gave her the freedom to accept or reject any of his teachings. Although he might trick her from time to time to keep her on her toes, he never tried to force her into doing anything against her will. Helen learned many things from Morya but probably the most important was how to identify an inner white magician or being from a black one. As she tells it, "A black magician will promise you the world and tell you exactly what you want to hear to get you to do what they want. A white magician tells you what you need to know and never promises anything other than hard work and the necessity for greater surrender to the Christ."

Until her training with Esther, Helen's clairvoyant and clairaudient perception of the spiritual realm had been free flowing and without much structure. The more she trained, the more her inner vision, hearing and intuitive skills increased and became an integral part of her communications with others. During a ten-day stay and training period with Esther in August, her vision took another leap. From the first day she arrived she worked on the inner with Esther. What this meant was that she "looked in" or viewed clairvoyantly, the action and effects of Esther's prayers and Ray work on the inner spiritual planes. At first she was very hesitant because of her lack of formal training and was not quite sure of what she was seeing. With each day she became more confident but found that the work drained her physical energy level so much that she could only work for an hour without a period of rest. By the end of her stay, it was difficult for her to do any inner work at all.

This lack of clairvoyant stamina and focus really troubled Helen because she inherently knew the immense value of clearance work. It was a gift from God in that it gave her practical access to the actual sources of spiritual energy, information and inner plane activities that she had previously lacked. Part of her problem was the challenge and adjustment of learning how to focus her attention in these dimensions. Although to the casual observer, sitting around in a meditative state with your eyes closed might not look tiring or difficult, the effort to train and use these faculties is enormous. It is much like physical training for a sport or the intellectual conditioning of the mind.

Helen had an automatic and inherent attunement to inner plane life. She intuitively knew that this focus was the key to understanding the energy essence of life through her own individual God Self. She had such a powerful curiosity about the workings of these dimensions that she became easily caught up in its activity, at the expense of her outer physical body and life. In this respect she was contributing to her own difficulties.

Feeling drained or energized by clearance work also can relate to your partner who is holding the active energy pole with you through the work. What Helen later discovered was that some of what she was seeing and reporting upset Esther. Through their work together, Esther was beginning to see Helen as a High Initiate who received considerable attention from the Ascended Masters. As her teacher, Esther felt threatened by this reality. When these feelings surfaced, Esther lost her inner balance and outer objectivity and her ability to protect Helen from certain inner plane energies that would cause harm to her bodies and drain her vital energy.

Also, through their clearance relationship, Esther tried to restrain or control the level of Helen's inner perception to conform to what Esther already knew or wanted verified for herself. Esther's psychic attempts to control Helen in this respect contributed to Helen's challenge in learning and to her fatigue. But Helen did gain exposure and experience through the process which was extremely valuable.

It was during this August 1968 visit to Los Angeles that Helen became conscious of taking "inner energy initiations." Initiations are cycles and levels of increases in energy, above and beyond that which a normal life span would encounter. This energy is invoked through the commitment to transmutation, whereby the higher "creative fires" pass through and change an initiate's inner bodies. Through each of these increases, energy infiltrates into the physical body usually hitting the weakest points (many times involving the heart). The effects of these increases can also cause extreme psychological difficulties in the consciousness and life of the individual. About initiatory energy and its effect on her life, Helen said "Physical situations occurred that forced me to release from my life that which I thought I couldn't live without, and added to my life that which I thought I couldn't tolerate or live with."

To Helen, energy initiations were simply final exams to find out how well and to what degree she could make practical application of learned theory or information. In the material world, testing or licensing is required when working with potent forces of nature such as electricity or radioactive materials, because of their inherent danger to human life. There is no difference when it comes to the more potent unseen spiritual energies. These creative forces of God's Divine Love and Will are working behind and directing the form activities of the natural world and the life of the human body. There are certain energy protocols in the spiritual world which demonstrate practical experience and abilities with these forces. Helen realized it is possible to die from contact or exposure to these energies if one is not properly prepared, tested and functional in dealing with them. She was definitely moving into a more serious level of her training and commitment on the Initiatory Path.

Helen continued her training and study which kept her traveling between Alabama, Colorado and California. One day, during one of Esther's classes in Los Angeles, her consciousness was drawn out her body and she found herself on inner realms with the Cosmic Christ. While in that energy state, she was given, and accepted, her next task to fulfill and the energy resources necessary for the work. Before she returned to her body, she also talked with the Ascended Master Saint Germain about what was happening to her at this time. Since Saint Germain was the sponsor for the I AM Activity, this was an especially important communication for Helen. Besides his relationship with the group activity, it was commonly accepted and well documented within many old esoteric, metaphysical and spiritual movements that when Saint Germain was in embodiment, he had lived on for centuries without dying. At this time, Helen could think of no better reference or guide for herself and wanted to get to know him better.

After this event, Helen began to realize that even without Esther she had immediate and personal access to the Masters and could talk to them at any time. Although Esther provided a structure and framework for her learning and training, Helen was gaining independence through her own internal and independent experience. This was validating to her and when she returned home to Alabama, she felt spiritually invigorated and more practically grounded than before. Once again she felt ready to move forward in her work and, of course, had no idea what this would mean.

The activities in Helen's inner reality began to invade her daily life. Masters began showing up to talk to her at the most inconvenient times and places and her dream life became an active stage for her to hear and see things about herself that needed attention. There was one particular dream she had shortly after returning from Los Angeles that deeply troubled her. In that dream she was told that she did not know how to love. At first this information seemed entirely contrary to her and what she felt like was her very loving and compassionate nature. Her need to understand, exactly, what this meant became the focus of her daily work and meditation. As God revealed the meaning of this dream to her, she began to realize that it was the depth and breadth of her immense love of people and life that was her problem. She always wanted the best of everything for people and automatically offered her love as a bridge to that end. The problem was that this pattern also served as an opening for her to take into her body the pain, agony and disappointment of those for whom she felt compassion and wanted to help.

This discovery was hard on Helen. She did not want anyone to suffer or to be unaware of the power and magnificence of God's Grace in their life. But she knew that taking their suffering into her body was not the answer. God showed her that she had to learn to love in a way that allowed others their own experience of pain and suffering.

From experience, Helen knew that pain and suffering were life's most powerful defenses against change on the physical plane. Because of this, the human orientation is to avoid them at all costs. But from a spiritual orientation, human pain and suffering have always been the true agent of change and progress in the world. It takes the power of impersonal love and objectivity in matter to experience pain and still know that, in truth, it is the result of our own limitations in consciousness and not God forsaking us. The energy of the Christ is our deliverance from that pain and represents God's Grace or bridge to a new way of living with infinite possibilities.

As she continued to observe these insights in regards to her own behavior with others, she realized that people must know and live this reality for themselves. If not, it has no power in their lives. Furthermore, she learned that true compassion is knowing that only God can deliver others from pain through the power of their own faith. She learned that temporarily she could help by extending to others the power of her faith, but at some point Christ love compelled her to step aside to let God's energy do the redeeming. This was true, even though a person might not receive redemption and continue to suffer, or even die.

When this kind of "tough love" approach is practiced with loving understanding from one's own personal experience, it is a powerful support to those who must face themselves and find salvation from within. But, if applied coldly, harshly and devoid of love, it can also invoke and strengthen the very negative psychic energy and suffering that it is intended to help alleviate.

Helen had difficulty with these realizations. Although it was painful to her, she experienced and received deeper levels of Divine Love and Will to carry out her job. She found ways to modify her expression of love in order to give others the freedom needed to develop their own connection with the Christ. With this understanding and subsequent changes in her life, a major cornerstone fell in place for her impending role as spiritual teacher.

# Chapter Two

Although Helen's commitment to place herself totally in God's care was firm, she was still working her faith through all levels of her consciousness and body to make it immutable. When she first felt abdominal pain in November 1968, she initially passed it off as an internal energy adjustment and went on with her life. Finally the pain got so severe she couldn't tolerate it anymore. As her previous experience with doctors proved negative at best, she wanted to avoid consulting them at all costs. She knew she needed to take some kind of faith-affirming physical action within herself to invoke God's healing energy to take care of the problem.

Helen tried many home remedies for abdominal problems. But none of these seemed to work. In desperation, she decided to try an iodine-based remedy that she had heard about. To find out more about it and the exact formula for the solution, she phoned the local hospital emergency room for information. As the story goes, apparently the person she spoke to kept her on the phone long enough for a hospital rescue crew to get to her house to check her out. They thought she was going to attempt suicide! She never did find out about the iodine remedy and the pain only got worse.

So it was in this state that Helen relented and made the decision to see a doctor. The x-rays showed she had gallstones and the doctor scheduled an operation to surgically remove them. Reluctantly, Helen agreed to treatment. When the doctor made his rounds the night before her surgery, Helen told him that she was going to "think away" the gallstones and that the surgery would not be necessary. He was quite upset and before he left he told her he believed this was impossible!

Later as she lay in bed praying and directing God's healing energy into the stones, she felt a slight burning sensation in her abdomen which gradually turned quite hot. She began to perspire heavily and then suddenly, as if a fever had broken, the heat disappeared and so did her abdominal pain. While this was going on, she said she could see a laser-like device directing a ray of energy directly into the stones until they disappeared completely from her gallbladder.

The next morning she told the doctor what happened and that the gallstones were gone. Although doubtful, he ordered additional x-rays taken before the operation. She already knew what the results would be. Later when he returned to her room with the x-ray results, he told her that there must have been something wrong with the original x-rays because the new ones showed no gallstones. With this experience, she knew she was firmly in God's hands.

81

In these incidents, Helen was testing her own faith in what God told her and promised her. She did this automatically and daily in many small ways. As her confidence in her faith and trust grew, she expanded the possible ways to test herself.

In the late 1960s, Helen owned a high-performance Pontiac GTO. She said driving this car gave her a sense of freedom and added "spice to her life." Often she drove it with reckless abandon. She saw her car as a symbolic representation of her physical body and used it in a way to further break up unconscious patterns and restrictions. In one of her discussions with God, she was assured that no harm would come to her. One day while driving she decided to test her faith in God to protect her from physical danger and others around her. She pushed the accelerator to the floor and began to speed in and around other cars. This was not on a downtown or busy city street but rather on a rural stretch of a US highway. At one point she lost control of the car as her wheels lost traction. She skidded through traffic and narrowly missed crashing into a metal culvert before the car miraculously came to rest on the side of the road.

Some may say this was dumb luck or that Helen showed reckless regard for her life and others. But to Helen, this practical exercise was what she needed to anchor another level of unshakable knowing that she would be protected. Each level of Helen's willingness and ability to surrender, lifted huge psychological burdens from her that made it possible to proceed with added faith in God's Plan for her. As a conscious act and symbol of always placing herself in God's care, she chose never to wear a car seat belt. Several years later she stopped driving almost completely and surrendered her safety to God through others.

In working on her own transmutation, Helen found that every part of her physical life was an external symbol and expression of her Higher Self. Conversely then, the fastest way to clearly see and change hidden internal patterns and structures was to put enough real pressure on them to force them to reveal themselves. One effective way she dealt with this was by intentionally changing the way she acted, dressed, and interacted with people in her life to challenge her patterns of conformity. Through the disturbance this caused within her subconscious, she stood a chance of identifying and changing things about herself that normally eluded her when personality controls were active. This was the essence of Helen, always cutting across the grain of conventional human behavior and social norms. It seems like all of her life, she lived contrary to the way people around her lived, who were doing everything possible to maintain peace, tranquility and harmony.

Although her behavior never physically threatened or harmed anyone's life or property, it did challenge and sometimes intimidate people who knew her or were around her. Having to live with the unconscious reactions, rejection and general sense of isolation was not easy for Helen. But she never let on. These were the very characteristics that qualified her to be a good teacher. She accepted the terms of her life unconditionally. For those genuinely interested in pursuing the freedom of Spirit, she was a true inspiration.

For a period of about nine months, Helen had been gradually withdrawing her attention and attendance away from the Colorado group. The group hierarchy within this activity, with its methods, rituals and practices, had become too restrictive for her. Helen was grateful to both of its spiritual leaders for what she had learned and experienced. Her training had prepared her well to stand and teach on her own. But she had grown beyond what the organization could offer her. So in September 1968, Helen resigned. Disconnecting from this entity was not an easy transition, and it turned out to be Helen's next crucial lesson and experience in how spiritual ritual and energy can be misused.

Apparently, her departure had a deep impact on the leadership of the group. So much so that they began to see Helen as their enemy. When the leadership found out that Helen was also giving dictations, all psychic hell broke loose. At this point they considered her a false prophet and a direct challenge to their line of authority from the Ascended Masters. This view of Helen had no basis in fact. She did not try to take students with her nor did she try to malign anyone towards the spiritual leadership or the organization. Helen just needed to be free of the encumbrance of a spiritual activity that she was unable to support wholeheartedly.

From their overreactions, one might assume that they were afraid of what she might reveal about them or how she might do damage to them. This fear grew to the point where the entire group was told to decree against Helen. These were not just decrees to disconnect her completely from their energy stream but rather malicious and vicious projections towards Helen and her life.

What started out as a simple resignation turned into a psychic battle. Had they left her alone and given her the freedom to be without interference in her life, Helen would have gone on and not looked back. However, the strength of the group projection of negative energy towards her was such that Helen was forced to take action to protect herself. Hostile projections can be dangerous and debilitating at many levels. A psychic, inner attack can be just as vicious and dangerous as if the aggressors are physically present in your life and trying to physically harm you.

Helen believed the source of the group's reaction to her sprang from their disagreement with her regarding "spiritual purpose." In essence, this was a power struggle to control Helen's inherent right to the freedom of her own individual direction and expression of God's energy. It was not in Helen's nature to battle with others, but when pressed she could be ruthless and relentless.

During this unfortunate state of war (which went on for many months, possibly a year), Helen became a formidable warrior and learned how to stand in the power and authority of her own God Self in the flames of God's Divine Justice. She did this by asking God to handle the situation according to the laws of karma of all those involved. Usually the karma between people has been working for many, many lifetimes. The energy of Divine Justice is incorruptible. It has the ability to synthesize and review the totality of these experiences between people over time in a role similar to that of a legal court system on the physical plane. However, It does this with inherent accuracy in the spirit of justice. Ultimately, what this meant was that Helen surrendered the outcome of her situation with the Colorado group to God to be equitably resolved at a higher level. She did not expect it necessarily to go in her favor but rather according to the higher laws of karma and justice.

This reality of true justice often staggers human comprehension and its instinctive patterns of believing that it can escape or avoid final accountability for its actions and behavior. Believing and trusting in this spiritual resource was an incredible support for Helen. What she learned about herself through this crisis along with her ability to release the outcome to God, helped her further commit her life and surrender to Divine Justice.

# Chapter Three

By January 1969, the group of people who regularly stopped by her house in Huntsville grew in size and commitment to the point where they asked her to be their spiritual teacher. These people were around Helen's age, in their mid-to late thirties, and came primarily from personal growth and self-improvement groups. The techniques they used and applied for themselves came out of meditation, yoga, group encounter and Transactional Analysis.

Helen said that the coalescing energy of this group came from the fact that most of these people felt trapped by the circumstances and events of their life. She also stated that the primary level of energy focus for this group was mental. That does not mean there weren't those among them who had great depth of feeling, sensitivity or intuition. It just meant that their interest in the material she offered was mainly intellectual. Most were raised as Christians, but at one time or another, each had become disenchanted with the traditional teachings of Christianity.

The late 1960s and early 1970s were a time of considerable personal and national soul-searching. Although much of the public attention during this period focused on the younger and more visible population of protesters and activists, there were many adults who were quietly, behind the scenes, questioning the religious, moral and social values of their generation. Where college students and young adults acted out their challenge to the establishment in the outer world, this older group turned their attention inward to look at themselves internally. As a result, many became dissatisfied with the quality and circumstances of their lives and work.

This was the cross-section of people who sought out Helen for their teacher. They were struggling against the current of traditional religious, social and family values by which they were raised and with which they could no longer identify. In breaking from their previous religious conditioning, some had become agnostic and even atheists in their quest for a new and more meaningful life and identity. Of course, deep down inside, they loved and embraced God but the religious and moral values of their upbringing were either too limited or had failed to guide and inspire them with the promise they so genuinely desired.

Helen said, "In truth, I've never met a person, even an atheist, who at the core of their unconscious being did not believe in some concept of a divine source of life." In fact she considered both agnosticism and atheism as positive spiritual transition periods rather than as expressions of negativity towards God. In these periods, she believed various aspects of an individual's existing concepts

85

of God go through a death process to prepare them to discover God in new ways. However, to do this people must have the freedom to test and live their beliefs without condemnation or interference from anyone else. She saw everyone's life as their religion and their individual path back to God. God's mission for her was quite clear and comforting in that He wanted her to help others consciously find their true God beauty within. This discovery would then show them their own way home.

Perhaps one reason these individuals were attracted to Helen was that in her break from her own fundamental Christian roots, she had never lost her deep and abiding faith in God. Rather than rejecting God with the traditional belief system, she asked God to help free her from the form and structure of her past. This led Helen to a new and revolutionary level of consciousness where she could have the freedom to know and experience the energy of God as It spoke to her. So in this respect, Helen was a radiant spiritual bridge for these people to rediscover God in themselves and in life around them.

From her leadership work in the Colorado activity, Helen had learned the power of group decrees and had already introduced this new group formally to this energy ritual. This apparently gave everyone a new regard for what spiritual life could be and inspired new insights as to how to transform their spiritual focus and orientation. As her studies with Esther progressed, she brought back to them the latest tools from Esther's chart and clearance work to help support their desire for change and transmutation.

Transmutation, in theory, is really much more centralized in our culture than most people realize. In esoteric wisdom, alchemy was the process used to convert or transmute base metals into gold or silver. In religion, it is God's Grace or the Divine that will redeem humankind and render the material world sublime through transfiguration. In psychology, it is the goal of every practitioner to help individuals transform life-debilitating and painful experiences towards a liberating wholeness of being. The purpose is to reclaim one's sense of self-direction, independence and functional balance in life. Helen's students learned the essence of this work and struggled to internalize its meaning to help redirect their lives.

In contrast to Helen, Esther, being much older, had been teaching for years and had recently been searching for ways to revitalize her group and the spiritual lives of its members. The I Am Reading Room was a much older activity with an average age in the mid-to upper fifties. Although a generation removed from the Huntsville group and with similar Christian roots, they differed in a most important way. First, many had spent most, if not all, of their adult lives, getting free from their early religious conditioning, and as students of the Ascended Masters they were learning to follow the Light of their own God or Christ Self. They had been through the trials of public scrutiny through the parent organization called "The I AM Activity" during the 1930s and 1940s. They had suffered through the travails of the organization's fragmentation after the death of its founders. (Esther's group was one of many which splintered off from the original activity.)

Through it all, they had stuck with their deep belief in the work taking place on Earth by the Spiritual Hierarchy of Ascended Masters. Over the years they had forged a deep personal commitment to silently serve the Light of God through their lives. They were well versed in Esther's chart work and had been doing decrees for decades. In a way, they were new agers before the "New Ageism" of the latter part of the century took hold. Along with other successor spiritual groups from nineteenth century spiritualism, they had worked hard to keep the fires of their spiritual activities alive and burning until the torch was passed to future movements.

The struggle to do this had left them depleted individually and collectively. Added to this was a promise of physical ascension made by Saint Germain (conveyed through their messenger) for all those who followed the prescribed path in their activity. For many, the years and diligent efforts of selfless work and dedication towards this promise of physical ascension, now seemed to be elusive and fading.

In order to keep on with their difficult and noble mission, the group had withdrawn into a kind of self-protective shell of spiritual superiority and crystallized armor in regards to the rest of the world around them. After all, they believed they were "the chosen ones" of the Master Saint Germain and of the Planetary Spiritual Hierarchy to do this important work to save the Earth and humankind. Even though their original intent might have been valid, the strength of their resulting orientation towards self-protection and superiority had isolated the individuals from the very energy they were trying to keep alive and express to the world. They had become resistant to change and therefore inadvertently and unintentionally had become bound or captured by their own creation. Their group needed new life and energy to revive them. As Esther saw it, this would come through Helen.

Helen's life and spiritual orientation had always been one of synthesis. This came from a deep and active faith in God's power to lead and transform her life as well as from a practical knowledge and receptivity to transformation techniques. She now found herself involved in two different groups on different sides of the country who were, in many ways, at opposite ends of the spectrum. Helen was caught in the middle between these two entities and struggled to find the necessary synthesis within herself to actively participate in each and to literally be able to move back and forth between them.

As Helen continued her work in Los Angeles, it became apparent to Esther that she was not just another student. Helen's inner plane proficiencies grew and flourished, and she began giving short dictations from the Masters to her group in Huntsville and to the I AM Reading Room students in Los Angeles (with Esther's support and approval). This added a whole new dimension to Helen's life. Previously when she spoke with any Master, it had been in private and had been a two-way communication. Now with the public dictations, the Masters took over her physical faculties to speak directly through her. When this happened, they wanted her to step aside as a kind of observer while they controlled her brain and nervous system with their energy. This was very distressing to Helen. She had to find ways of guarding her individual energy channel and identity while offering herself in service to a number of Masters wanting access to students through her.

As 1969 ended, the intensity, depth and frequency of giving dictations increased. The Masters who wanted to communicate through her continued to invade her life as did the student reaction to her new role of giving dictations. The potent spiritual energies delivered through these dictations was a strain for Helen and the effects were debilitating to her physical body. This was especially true for her nervous system which was going through changes in order to better carry and express the increasingly higher forces she was invoking through her work. One result was excessive nerve sensitivity. Helen became so physically sensitized that even the normal activities and noises of life and of her child playing around the house became so harsh and painful that it frequently pushed her over her threshold of being able to cope.

Her hope for a private and domestic life at home with Jeffery was diminishing at an alarming rate. As this happened, Helen grew increasingly concerned for him and his well-being. Her commitment to her service to God's Energy and Light had infused her to the point where she could not even imagine life without it. But what about Jeffery? More and more as he was growing, his needs were changing. She knew deep within her heart that at some level she had no right as a parent to subject her child to this kind of life and energy. But for his sake and her commitment to motherhood, she tried to keep up some semblance of normality. But as 1969 turned into 1970 this became nearly impossible.

# Chapter Four

By 1970, Helen was regularly giving dictations to the Los Angeles group. The Master Morya continued to give her individual guidance and support from the inner planes. Although he was her spiritual sponsor and teacher, in a strange way, he was her student as well. Increasingly, it became apparent to him and the other Masters, that Helen had access to levels of Cosmic Christ energy that went beyond their abilities. When she connected with this alignment, she could be quite unpredictable. Just because she had contact with so called "Ascended Masters" and even gave their dictations, she did not worship or elevate them as gods.

Her spiritual connection to God was through her individual connection with the Cosmic Christ and Its power through the Holy Spirit. The Masters were not the last word on anything to Helen. Everything they told her or wanted her to do, immediately she took to God for verification. Because of this, she seemed insolent to many of these Beings. To others of them, she was downright threatening to their "elevated" power and authority with their positions in Hierarchy. Although Esther's heart was open to Helen and she had followed her own spiritual guidance in working with her, more and more her sympathies began to fall with the group in Hierarchy who felt challenged and threatened by Helen.

Esther knew at the time she met Helen that her organization had become stagnant and crystallized in its rituals and operation, and for a time she was receptive to Helen's practical ability to encounter the patterns of unconsciousness in the people and in the entity of the group. So, with Esther's blessing, Helen began doing outrageous things to shock this group out of their spiritual doldrums. Her shock treatment included, but was not limited to, showing up for dictations before the group in miniskirts or hot pants and boots. In these dictations she spoke practically and directly avoiding glamorous language and often resorted to swearing. This outraged many of the members because Helen did not meet their strict requirements of what a spiritual messenger should be. This was Helen's intention. Their reactions were the potential openings to release their glamorous expectations and requirements.

Helen went through a lot of transmutation just to be able to behave this way publicly. Her preferred manner and dress was quite conventional and professional. The conscious, subconscious and unconscious reaction to her behavior was severe and at times hostile, and had quite an effect on her. Often on her weekend trips to Los Angeles, she vomited on the way out and back in the airplane lavatory. She said that while in Los Angeles she hardly ate anything substantial yet always came back having gained weight. Several times she came back after a three-day visit about ten pounds heavier.

In the meantime, the members of Helen's Huntsville group were also progressing with their studies and training. They had come a long way since early 1969 when she first accepted them as students. By early 1970, Helen and the group filed nonprofit incorporation papers in Alabama to be known as The Children of Light Society. When Helen first found out that she was to start The Children of Light Society, she thought that her involvement in it might last from six weeks to six months at the most. As those periods passed, she thought it would maybe only last for two years. In time she had to face the fact that her work would not end anytime soon. This was very difficult for her and she writes about it as follows:

"This was the most awful thing in the world to me. The one thing I knew I needed was the freedom to think my own thoughts within my own internal framework. I didn't realize just how deeply and thoroughly I thought things through for myself. When I told God or others that I believed in something or when I made a commitment, my thinking on the matter set in motion an internal alignment and process that got me mentally, emotionally and physically ready to embody my belief and carry out my commitment. I thought everyone did the same. But my experience with the student group forced me to face the fact that most people believe they mean what they say but don't have all their eggs together to follow through and act on what they say. This meant I would have to set disciplines to help people develop their own internal process of alignment."

"This was unpleasant to me because the last thing I wanted to do was to teach anyone anything. By even attempting to teach, I thought I would insult their intelligence. It was hard for me to accept that not only was I not insulting their intelligence, but that most of the time they had no idea what I was talking about. You see, I was forced by God all the way to go beyond my personal desires and preferences. In spite of myself, as it turns out, it was the greatest education I could have imagined."

Helen told her Huntsville group that if she was to be the spiritual leader and head of The Children of Light Society, they would have to accept her setting the spiritual and practical direction of the organization. She was direct and honest with them from the beginning. Helen did not consider a spiritual activity a democratic organization with the board of directors telling the leader how to do the job. If they did not like her leadership the board could always remove her. If they refused to follow her direction she would resign.

With Helen's various group activities it became almost impossible for her to continue working a full-time job and shuttle back and forth between Huntsville and Los Angeles. Helen asked the group to demonstrate their commitment to her by finding a way to pay her a salary so she could leave her job at Marshall. This would enable her to devote the time and energy needed to fulfill her commitment to the Christ and to them as their teacher. To meet this need, one particular student stepped forward to guarantee a monthly salary which made it possible for Helen to quit her job. However, this was only the first obstacle of many for her to face on the way to making The Children of Light Society a reality and to meet her commission in the Christ.

After forming the organization, it did not take long for a few individuals in the group to begin thinking, feeling and acting like they knew best how to set up the Society and how to run it for Helen. She said that when this started, "It was like being in the middle of a street fight with their intellectual faculties and egos acting as switchblades, slashing me to pieces." She knew within herself that she could have easily stood toe to toe with their mental forcefields and most likely defeated them at their own game. However, Morya told her that for the good of the work and for her own growth she should not defend herself.

As always, she followed this guidance and stepped back, knowing that it was the right thing to do. This did not mean though that she did not suffer through their frequent mental assaults. Unbeknownst to them, this was really of great assistance to Helen in learning how to be selfless and dispassionate for her future work. In addition, their mental forcefields were also of great assistance in helping to break up the crystallization in the I AM Reading Room group when they traveled with her to Los Angeles.

In Los Angeles, things were going from bad to worse. The relationship between Esther and Helen was quite strained and had escalated towards a confrontation. Because of the potent energy and integrity that Helen brought to her work as well as her mastery in giving dictations and doing clearance, Esther's own sense of authority to lead "her" group was challenged, and Esther's commitment and willingness to revive the group was waning.

The first disagreement between them came over clearance work. For years, Esther had controlled this process herself by being "the one" who directed the energy and training for only a few loyal followers. Students and members of the group were required to have all clearance work done by Esther thus creating a dependency on her. Helen believed that clearance was just like prayer and decreeing, and should be readily available to any and all who wanted to use it in their life. She felt called to teach it like any other spiritual technique or principle so that others might have the freedom to use and develop their own power and authority in God's energy.

Helen lived and practiced the Christ principle of prayer and knew that when she asked anything of God, in the Christ's name, it was given. To her, that was the whole essence of Christ's redeeming energy. Everyone's birthright is to have a direct Christ relationship to God through their faith, prayer, meditation or any other spiritual technique like clearance. She believed individuals should have access without the requirement that they go through some intermediary authority.

The second issue was really the last straw for Esther and led to the break up of the Los Angeles group. This related to the fact that Helen's relationship with the Ascended Masters had eclipsed that of Esther. Before Helen, Esther had been the one who held the connection with the Masters (although she never gave dictations). She was the one who gave out instructions she had received for the others to follow. However, more and more it was Helen to whom the Masters spoke and gradually it was she to whom they also began to give their directives.

As threatening and challenging as this was to Esther's sense of authority with her group, she apparently was able to support Helen's leadership role, for a while, for the good of the group. But there was one particular instruction from a Master which Esther could not tolerate - that Helen was to take over the job as group leader of the I AM Reading Room with Esther assisting her. Esther's reaction to this information drove a wedge between her and Helen with sufficient force to divide the students and put the group's future in serious doubt. Battle lines were drawn with students lining up behind one or the other and the breakup of the I AM Reading Room activity began.

Where as for many years Esther had been happy as the spiritual head of this group, being the leader of anything was not attractive to Helen. However, she had followed God's instructions and guidance for too many years to give it up now. So once she verified her instructions with the Christ, she moved ahead with all the courage and determination she could muster to fulfill her given purpose. Esther was voted out by the I AM Reading Room Board and steps were taken for this group to become part of The Children of Light Society, under Helen's spiritual leadership. Helen took no enjoyment in Esther's dismissal and wished her and her supporters well.

The hectic months leading up to the Children of Light incorporation as well as the aftermath, continued to take a toll on Helen's life with Jeffery. As more people met with Helen and attended classes in their home, Jeffery was having to take a back seat to her students. Even though they were friendly and loving towards him, it was evident there might come a time when he would feel emotionally abandoned and possibly damaged by the energy activities of his mother's life.

As Helen assessed her role in his life, she realized she continued to be distressed by the fact that for these past five years he had missed the guidance of a father in his life. Now, as he prepared to enter his teenage years, he especially needed this masculine influence. Also, it was painfully clear to Helen that in her own desire for freedom she might have given him too much freedom. As a child, he needed a minimum amount of constant, reliable structure and discipline on which to build a solid foundation for his later life. In addition, she did not feel it was right to hold him captive to her beliefs, faith and calling. She could not make that decision for him!

However, it was too painful to consider giving him up to his uncle Glenn, who had never let up on pressuring Helen to that end. By mid-1970, the Holy Spirit told her she was to move to Los Angeles and that she should begin preparations. This was a major point of no return for Helen which forced her to accept that her life was no longer her own. As she reviewed her life with Jeffery and considered the impending move, Helen knew within her heart that the best thing for him was to go and live with his uncle in Medina.

Knowing the truth of something in your heart does not mean that your heart doesn't break. She wrestled with this inner knowing for some time and as usual she took her pain and anguish to God. For probably the first time in her life, Helen tried to negotiate with God. She begged for just one more year with Jeffery before she had to give him up. God told her that there was no more time and that, as she wrote in her notes, "Jeffery would not survive my future life and if I did not do it now, I would wander in the desert for the rest of my life."

There was no way to explain adequately to Jeffery why she could not keep him with her. How do you sit down and explain to your eleven-year-old son that he can no longer be with you, that he must go somewhere else to live? There were so many things she wanted to tell him about life in general and her life specifically, but he was too young. Her heart ached to be able to share herself totally with him but that would have to wait until he was older (although she was afraid that by that time she would have lost him completely and he would not be interested). She always did her best to explain things to him in a language and in the context of the life that he knew. First Jeffery had lost his father and now he was to lose his mother! All that she could do was turn this over to God.

Although Helen did not really get along with Glenn or his wife, she had no doubt as to Glenn's genuine love for and commitment to Jeffery. She knew in her heart that Glenn would give Jeffery what he needed to grow up with an integrated strength of body, mind and spirit. Helen pledged to Glenn not to interfere with his parenting of Jeffery and committed to help support Jeffery's life with them financially, which she did faithfully throughout the years. As Helen left Medina without Jeffery that summer, she said it felt like her heart was being ripped out of her chest. She didn't think she could go on. She could not imagine life without him!

The social and family condemnation Helen had to face for such an act was potent and the pain unimaginable. She knew that the case against her would eventually begin to affect the way Jeffery felt about her and also might turn him against her. Her worst fears were confirmed the next summer when Jeffery came to visit for a few weeks. In only one year, his whole orientation towards her had turned negative. Although she had prepared herself for him to be hurt, she had believed that somehow their deep bond of love would enable them to make the transition to a new relationship before any permanent damage could take hold. Although she knew beyond a doubt that Glenn was good for Jeffery, she also knew that he was a negative influence on her relationship with him.

There was nothing she could do about Jeffery's attitude towards her that summer of 1971 or in the future, for that matter. Helen never tried to control the way anyone thought or felt about her. She knew that if she tried to defend herself it would only make things worse. She also had to trust that God would get Jeffery through it and would turn this painful event in his life into something positive for him. There was no other way through the pain than to surrender her son to God's care and keeping.

# Chapter Five

After her heart-wrenching experience with Jeffery, Helen thought her major testing period was over and she was ready to move forward with her life and work. Little did she know at the time that her testing had only begun. During the balance of 1970 and for most of 1971, Helen split her time between Huntsville and Los Angeles. There was much to do to wind up her life in Alabama in preparation for her move. Then there was also the matter of finding a way to blend the two student groups while personally learning how to assert herself in spiritual leadership. This was a challenging transition for Helen and her students. She did not feel comfortable having even one person hanging on her every word for some divine inspiration. Now she had a large group of people looking to her for spiritual guidance.

Helen worked diligently at the task of integrating the two student groups which made up The Children of Light Society. She had to find a way to help free all of the people involved from their respective group entities that held them bound to their previous conditioning. Her love of God and her willingness to completely surrender to the Christ were the radiance which linked this coalition of people. The strength and depth of Helen's spiritual life and her ability to live Christ principles in the face of radical changes in her life acted as the bridge of unity. She was honest, direct and without question always did what she said she would do.

Although well read, Helen always taught from her own practical experience in living the concepts contained in the books she and her students studied. It would have been a lot easier on her had she only taught spiritual theory. This was because she took the full brunt of the students' attention on her and their psychic reaction to her internalization of the material she taught. She offered her life experience as the focal point for their learning. Despite the price she paid, she believed this was in everyone's best interests.

The spiritual and initiatory principles Helen taught were by no means geared for the mainstream. For those whose orientation and attitude towards life was more traditional, there were already numerous established churches, organizations and groups to join and follow. From the start, her life and relationship to God was not only unique but was also quite challenging and threatening to collective social and religious values. Despite this opposition, Helen felt bringing God directly into everyday life was her calling and purpose for living.

In Helen's view, the challenge of human life is to learn consciously how to participate in spiritual creation. From this perspective, humanity stands as the bridge between the natural and spiritual worlds. Therefore the human kingdom, with its self-awareness and ability to think, is the key to changing the material world into the next level of spiritual manifestation. Although we have developed considerable human intelligence, the mind still is relatively undeveloped with regard to its creative potential to receive and use Divine consciousness. The obstacles to further development are centered in the human ego and negatively affect the way we think and feel about the role of God in our life. Many times in order to break these limitations, the transmutation process has to go against social convention to create a kind of divinely guided chaos out of which something new can emerge.

The challenge of integrating the Huntsville and Los Angeles groups was Helen's own brand of chaos. Little did she know she was about to receive some help. Back in her early involvement with the I AM Reading Room, she met a man named Brad Benton. However, it was not until the process of breaking up the group began that they were actually thrown together. This might seem like a strange way to describe two people getting together, but as Helen described the events of her life in Los Angeles, those were the words that came to mind. Brad's background was in business and accounting which enabled him to assist her by assuming responsibilities for the business aspects of the combined organization.

Brad and his wife, Lucille, were not only members of the I AM Reading Room, but also prominent leaders in the group. As a married couple, they were held up by Esther as a shining example of a successful spiritual union between a man and woman. This was because they strictly adhered to the form of the guidelines of marital propriety and student conduct given by the Ascended Masters. So, through Esther's sanctification of their relationship, Brad and Lucille inadvertently became the unconscious group symbols that form is more important than the Spirit behind it. This orientation contributed to the group stagnation and energy locks in the Reading Room.

As Helen worked with the Masters to bring these two groups together, she was told that she and Brad should be married as soon as possible. Further, she was told, the collective psychic reaction to Brad's divorce from Lucille and her marriage to Brad would break the group energy lock. In the long run, this action would enhance and unify the Children of Light and support spiritual growth individually for its members. This would help to set the stage for meeting the organization's spiritual purpose.

Even before Helen was told this, Brad had already made it quite clear to her that he was romantically interested in her and would leave Lucille. However, Helen had no desire or intention to be the reason for breaking up the marriage.

But Brad was serious and persistent. Considering this and then acting on it was not easy for Helen and, of course, it was devastating to Lucille. With Brad's consent and Lucille's reluctant cooperation, she now used the situation to send shock waves through the organization in order to break up as many restrictions and energy locks as possible.

Helen had the capacity in her nature and in her heart to receive and express exceptional amounts of love. She never did anything just because she was told to. It was her way to find her own reason and an authentic feeling within herself as motivation to move forward on anything she was asked to do by God. It was never a question with her that she would do it, but rather just how she would go about doing it. So while Brad's divorce was proceeding, she opened her heart to Brad in a way in which love flourished between them.

Brad was a very likable and magnetic person. He had dark rugged good looks with a very soft-spoken way about him. His eyes were powerful in that they expressed a kind of quiet intensity that was offset by his outwardly easygoing personality. His sense of humor was deep and subtle and he had a very warm way of relating to people. However, Brad was fourteen years older than Helen when they got together, and as it turned out, he was not physically well. Less than a year after their marriage, he suffered his first heart attack leading to constant battles with congestive heart failure. Because of this, he could not provide the kind of physical support to Helen that she needed. Often when she needed him the most, he was too ill with his own problems to help her through her own. So often, it was up to Helen, through her enormous faith in God, to see them both through the difficult physical periods of their life together.

Another significant person who entered Helen's life during this time was Ann, a young student of hers in California. From outward appearances, Ann had enjoyed a privileged life. After being raised a Roman Catholic, and cared for by family nannies, she felt somewhat unacknowledged by her parents in ways that she desired and needed growing up. With this internal pain came rebellion during her teenage years against parents who rarely expressed or extended much personal love towards her.

Unfortunately, when Ann was eighteen, her father died of cancer and then just a few years later, cancer also claimed her mother's life. Ann was left as the oldest of four children and the only daughter. Although she was close to graduating from college, she felt her life had no sense of direction or purpose. Even though she had a deep and abiding love of God, she was estranged from her Catholic upbringing with its restrictive doctrines and heavy-handed strictures. In April 1970, she narrowly escaped being caught bringing marijuana from Mexico into this country. In her prayers as she crossed the border, she promised God that if she were spared arrest and the consequences of her actions, she would change her life and rededicate it to God.

As Ann stated, "I was and I did." After graduating from college and during the summer of 1971, she was introduced to The Children of Light Society through neighbors in Santa Barbara, California. It was at a conference in Running Springs, when Ann was in her early twenties, that she first met Helen and experienced her first dictation from an Ascended Master. Attending this conference and witnessing the physical effects on Helen as she gave the dictation, was a turning point for Ann. She was stunned to see the effects of the energy, from the Master speaking through her, take over Helen's body as well as to see her body sharply jolt backwards when the dictation ended. She realized that if that energy could transform Helen's body, then it could surely change her own life. Ann continued to attend classes and became involved in group activities.

Later that year, Ann attended another conference in Tennessee. During this time, Helen became sick and Ann was told by an "inner voice" to offer to return home with her to stay and help out. This was the beginning of a very long and close relationship between them. Ann was still struggling with the deep loss of both parents and her own sense of abandonment. With the intensity of her work and schedule, Helen needed care and support around the clock. At this time, neither knew that three years later, Ann would become a serious student, as well as Helen's trusted assistant, clearance partner and companion.

In time, Ann became known as Helen's adopted daughter and this lasted throughout their relationship of twenty-three years, which only ended with Helen's death. During this time, Ann never defaulted in her willingness to put Helen and her spiritual work above all else in her life. This required immense personal sacrifice and dedication to God.

# Chapter Six

Helen finally made her move to California in late 1971 and took a small apartment in Pasadena. Later, she and Brad moved into temporary quarters while the old I AM Reading Room house and headquarters was being redone after Esther had moved out. In the spring of 1972, she and Brad were at last able to settle into the refurbished headquarters. Brad's divorce was final in August 1972 and Helen and Brad were married the following month in a small private ceremony.

From the moment Helen and Brad moved in, their household was set up for student group living. In time, this also included Ann. Daily, Helen worked with individuals, taught classes, gave dictations and spent much of the day and night doing clearance or prayer work as directed by the Holy Spirit. Public church services were held in a chapel in the rear of the house and conferences were given twice a year. Oftentimes, it was necessary for her to travel to various parts of the country and North America to draw energy and direct inner work needed in those specific locations. With this lifestyle, she began to understand why she had been told that it would not be in Jeffery's best interests for him to continue living with her.

The group living arrangement was not Helen's preference. She felt this was a practical necessity in the way she trained serious students to give them a solid grounding before they went out to form their own groups. Everyone who trained in Helen's household learned the art and ritual of service as part of their training. They were never considered personal servants, as many have tried to convey. The truth of the matter was that the group living and training was probably harder on Helen than any of her students could have imagined. To always have people around and underfoot was a substantial sacrifice to her privacy and self-reliance.

Through the training of her students and reflection of her own life, Helen recognized that to most people, spirituality was relegated to off hours from "real" life and work. In many religious families she felt that rituals, such as mealtime blessings or grace, were regularly practiced but often done so routinely and automatically that they were devoid of any real depth of gratitude and appreciation for God's sustaining role in their life.

She observed that it was common for adults with heavy work and family responsibilities to believe or accept that their spiritual focus was not a priority or truly an essential part of their daily life. This happens because people feel that their life and what sustains that life arises purely from the visible, physical world, rather than actually coming through it from the spiritual realm. This kind of life orientation first deflects and then replaces the human connection to a living God reality. It promotes a feeling and identity of being separate from, rather than being inherently united with, the essence of God.

The very reality of our physical body demands that we must meet its most basic needs for food, water, shelter, clothing and security. Because of the physical nature of our world, most see these essential life ingredients coming from the external and natural world of matter all around us as well as from human invention, labor and willpower. Helen believed it was important to recognize that these elements came from the Energy of God to the natural world around us. As it relates to the human factor, she saw this coming from the individual God Selves within each of us.

It might sound as if this distinction is splitting hairs. But from Helen's perspective there is a huge difference in orientation. One is worshiping nature, the human potential and the matter of life rather than seeing it for what it is - simply a form for God's energy to us. Helen's attitude and orientation always was to celebrate the spiritual reality underlying and behind all objective physical form. In learning how to do this automatically, she practiced a state of being and living in continual prayer.

For Helen, feeling her depth of gratitude to God for life was completely natural. She found that the only way to help others reverse their material life orientation was to learn how to reorient and to requalify their life in the Spirit of the Christ. To do this, they must learn to see and to celebrate God's magnificent sustaining energy in the smallest and most automatic aspect of routine living. Helen said this was not easy. As children, most of us have been unconsciously, subconsciously and consciously conditioned to see and relate to God as something separate and apart from our physical world or visible life.

It was Helen's priority in training to give her students the opportunity and motivation to learn how to requalify their lives in the living Spirit of God. They had to relearn how to perform and carry out the behavior and activities they normally did automatically by learning how to consciously feel and see their life through God, as if for the first time. When one learns this and consciously practices it as a matter of routine, one becomes a point of Christ Light within the overall Christ Plan for humanity and the earth.

One component of this training was to learn how to prepare food infused or qualified with the Christ Spirit so that all who ate this food were not only nourished of body, but of Soul and Spirit. She taught her students how to qualify their bodily appearance, clothes, home, profession and recreation in this same way to nurture their spirituality in everyday life. With this kind of orientation, raising children, cleaning, shopping, working as a plumber, a doctor, a construction worker or whatever activity or profession one is actively living, the

Christ principle can extend the radiance of God's Grace to all those we love and come in contact with.

In living these transmutation principles, over time the tide of the preconditioned material orientation begins to yield to a new way of being. This new pattern unifies all life, not just in principle but in practice. It incorporates a spiritual purpose and dimension to the orientation of living. Rather than feeling depleted by the daily activities of life, one is filled with energy because of them.

The Children of Light Society continued to grow along with the various group activities. This increased to the point where Helen was offering conferences four times a year. When the I AM Reading Room split up, there were groups of students in various locations in the Los Angeles area that continued to accept Helen as their teacher. In addition to her own local group, Helen had students from these locations as well as students flying in from Huntsville to attend conferences or training. Helen now had a personal staff, in addition to Ann, to assist her and Brad with the various duties of cooking, cleaning, and the business details of running an organization. The travel work also became more frequent to the point where it was not unusual to have different groups continually taking off in different directions for the purpose of clearance and drawing energy.

In the spring of 1973, Helen and a group of students left for a "working trip" to Mexico and the Caribbean, returning across the full length of the United States-Canadian border. Although these locations might sound glamorous, these trips were anything but. They involved hard work with little sleep or time for leisure. It was during the trip to Mexico that Brad had his first minor heart attack, marking a period of declining health. This was hard on Helen as she was having her own physical difficulties to deal with.

Ever since 1968, when she began consciously taking energy initiations, Helen progressively experienced extreme changes taking place in her physical body. She had always been a rather healthy person and had a hearty physical constitution. But by early 1973, these changes started to become debilitating. To make matters worse, she was having to deal with the continuing battle on the inner planes with the breakup of the I AM Reading Room. Although the Board of Directors voted Esther out of her position and out of the organization, she remained bitter over this incident for years. She blamed Helen personally for this and was the cause of much disturbance and animosity directed towards Helen on inner planes. The intensity of this energy was quite potent and physically devastating. Constant clearance work was needed on just this one particular focus, not to mention many others.

It was sometime in 1974 that Helen was told by the Holy Spirit that she needed to move herself and the organization back to Alabama. By this time Helen's students were accustomed to the perpetual motion of changes of one kind or another. Although not entirely happy about the choice before them, most picked up their lives to follow her.

# PART FIVE:

# THE WORK

*Frederick R. Kipp*

# Chapter One

To further understand the spiritual foundation in Helen's life, it might be helpful to know more about The Children of Light Society (or The Church of the Living Light as it became known in 1975).

The Children of Light Society was the spiritual teaching organization established to fulfill Helen's commission to help people find, see and experience the beauty of their individual God Selves. Its goal was to do this through the activities of spiritual education and to assist others in living Christ principles in all aspects of temporal life. The "Light" in both names signifies the Light of the Christ revelation and Its transformative effect in the world and in all human life. As John says of the Christ in the Bible (John 1:9, King James version), "That was the true Light, which lighteth every man that cometh into the world." Although It might be called many different names around the world, Helen believed that this Light (divine energy, essence or illumination) is not exclusive to any one race, nation or religion, but is available to all people as their birthright. So she felt all humans coming into this world are "Children of the Light."

John goes on to say (John 1:10) that "He was in the world, and the world was made by him, and the world knew him not." To Helen this meant that the real mission of any Christ-based religious or spiritual organization is to help people find their own Christ revelation and to learn to live the Christ Principles and Light in their everyday life.

First and foremost from a universal standpoint, the Society acknowledged and accepted a Divine Trinity in God the Father, God the Son and God the Holy Spirit. In metaphysical terminology it is the First, Second and Third Logos, whereby the Word is the manifested deity of all humans. The Society introduced people to an impersonal and universal God as the underlying creative energy of all life expressing through humankind, the earth and the universe.

Although Helen saw an underlying Divine Creative Plan working its way through evolutionary cycles of physical manifestation, she believed the quality of all human life depends on the level of consciousness of our creative life in this energy of God. With this perspective, we all start as unconscious co-creators with God, struggling through cycles of death and rebirth in the evolutionary process, to become conscious co-creators in the Divine Creative Plan. From Helen's perspective, in essence, the only real sin in the world is the sin against the Holy Spirit or refusing to become conscious co-creators with God. All other sins are symptoms of this refusal.

In the Bible, the book of Genesis describes creation in a series of seven creative days and talks as if it is complete. This seems logical since everything

105

described in the creative days of Genesis is seemingly detectable by our physical sense perception. But the Bible also tells us that God is Spirit which is made manifest or takes form in the world. This leads us to suspect that there is a spiritual world which is not detectable by our physical senses. If that is true, then it is just as plausible that the "days of creation" represent ongoing periods, phases or cycles in a vast creative process which manifests God's idea of creation out of the spiritual world into matter.

According to esoteric Christianity and long-standing metaphysical spiritual wisdom, we are still living in a phase of these days of creation. Helen believed that creation is a continual, unfolding, creative process in God to prepare the physical bodies of humanity and the natural world to embody and express ever higher levels of God's energy, or consciousness, in dense physical matter. In order to accomplish this, the matter of the world is continuously undergoing creative change, or mutation, respective to the various cycles of evolution. The creative process to prepare dense physical matter to receive even the tiniest and simplest form of life took eons of evolutionary time, as did the evolution of the human physical body to receive the immortal human Soul.

Helen's perspective of creation brings the modern scientific theories of cosmology and evolution closer to conventional religious beliefs. Further, from a spiritual point of view, besides our corporal nature, human beings also have an immortal spiritual nature which did not evolve in the physical world as did our bodies. These natural human bodies are but material vehicles for our spirit to embody in the physical world.

The apostle Paul in his first epistle to the Corinthians (1 Corinthians 15:40) says that "There are also celestial bodies, and bodies terrestrial: but the glory of the celestial is one, and the glory of the terrestrial is another." By developing their spiritual awareness and clairvoyant and clairsentient faculties, members of the Society became introduced to and familiar with the inner realms of life as well as their own individualized spiritual nature. This happened gradually through time and with training, classes and specific disciplines designed to support their growth. With this inner perspective, they were then open to learning how to allow the Christ and Holy Spirit energies to transform the matter of their personality (the mental, emotional, etheric energy bodies and the physical body) into more refined receptacles for Christ expression in their life and the world.

The Children of Light Society acknowledged and accepted the individual Divine Trinity as the God Self, Christ Self and Personal Self within each human being. In metaphysical terminology they might be referred to as the Monad, the Spiritual Triad and the Embodying Ego. Because only a small part of the energy of this individual God Self is necessary to sustain physical life, most people are unaware of Its existence and the potential power in their lives. As a result, most look outside of themselves for God or meaning to their life.

In order to consciously find that Divine connection within us, Helen found it is necessary to develop countless ways and forms of learning and transmuting to allow the Christ to peel away the personal limitations that restrict consciousness. These underlying restrictions to conscious living are supported by stubborn evolutionary and material conditioning from our past and present lifetimes. They consist of superimposed layers of psychological records and archetypal patterns of the collective rules of human life and behavior. These are all barriers to our conscious awareness, knowing and expression of our spiritual birthright.

As reembodying Souls or Human Egos, we each share a part of the responsibility for the condition of the physical world in which we find ourselves living today. It is by surrendering to and following the inner guidance of the redeeming Christ presence within us that we are able to break the bondage of our material orientation in order to transmute the barriers of evolutionary consciousness as individuals or groups. She recognized that we are all immortal spiritual beings whose present temporal life conditions are a direct result of the karma of our past lives. In Christianity this is known as "original sin." Our physical lives are governed by the principles of reembodiment until we release and transmute our karma or our unconscious miscreations. When this happens, we become conscious co-creators in God's creative energy and thereby the architects of our future.

The organization's methods of teaching embraced religious, spiritual, metaphysical, psychological and philosophical concepts, beliefs and practices. It acknowledged and accepted that the wide diversity of religions, spiritual organizations and disciplines have their legitimate place within God's Creative Plan. The society also accepted the various sacred texts and teachings as divinely inspired but fallible by human interpretation.

With the assistance of the Ascended Masters and under the direction of the individual Christ Self, structure and support were given to open and develop the intuitive faculties enabling each person to freely interpret the teachings according to their own Christ Light. The price of following this Light is radical personality transmutation on the Initiatory Path. If this way of life is accepted and followed, then each person through their life becomes a point in matter through which the Christ Energy can flow to the world. Eventually, this path can lead to the Resurrection and the Ascension out of the lower human sensory orientation and into a conscious reunification with the Universal God.

In the Bible it is written in 1 Peter 2:9-10, that the Christ through Jesus established in all earthly people "a chosen generation, a royal priesthood, an holy nation, a peculiar people; that ye should show forth the praises of him who hath called you out of darkness into his marvelous light: Which in time past were not a people, but are now the people of God: which had not obtained mercy, but now have obtained mercy."

Therefore, Helen set about training a priesthood of believers and practitioners who wanted to know their inner God Reality and learn to express It in their life. Not only was this a practical necessity if the organization was to be successful, but it was also essential to prepare the future teaching and administrative leadership for when she would leave the organization. In the meantime, it was her job to help others recognize that every human being has the inherent privilege and responsibility of direct access to God through their own Higher or Christ Self.

Helen envisioned training a priesthood that would learn the essence and power of their individual Christ Self through the experience of daily living. Through these personal experiences they would teach people, formally and by example, how to become sustained and guided by their own Higher Selves. Their purpose was to become independent spiritual initiates, linked together as a priesthood, in service to the Christ purpose in the world. Although the personal sense of giving and contribution to humanity as a whole is satisfying and life enriching, an initiate's life is anything but glamorous. It is extremely hard work involving considerable personal sacrifice, many times extending into the loss of conventional family relationships, social acceptance and outer world activity.

# Chapter Two

By early 1973, the physical transmutation work on Helen's body was becoming severe. She found that each time the level of Christ energy increased in her consciousness, she experienced pain and difficulty in her body. Through these cycles, the Holy Spirit introduced her to the body consciousness underlying the biological human body. In the process of dealing with this limited consciousness, she learned that it was programmed only to direct biological activity. Because of this essential role in keeping the matter of the body alive, it resisted change at all cost. Therefore its reactions caused dysfunction, pain and physical mutation in the various systems of the body as it grudgingly gave way to the Christ energy. It was in this way that she discovered exactly how potent the energy was she was working in and the extent to which it speeds up the normal evolutionary process of the human, physical body.

The usual nature of the process in matter is to bring about physical change or mutation in small, biologically manageable increments over extended lengths of time. This pace allows time for increasing levels of Christ consciousness to gain practical, dense physical experience. This is necessary to reprogram the inherent human body consciousness and to recreate its dense form with this new level of creative energy. Where the evolutionary process incrementally increases energy cycles over long periods of time, the Initiatory Path brings about such drastic energy increases that rapid mutations occurred in her body in relatively short time periods.

By the fall of 1974, Helen and Brad had left Los Angeles and moved The Children of the Light Society to Guntersville, Alabama, a small southern town of 7,000. The Lake Guntersville area is a beautiful area just south of Huntsville. Although Huntsville is located in the Southern Christian Bible Belt, its national and international concentration in space technology makes its population mix somewhat more religiously tolerant than neighboring communities like Guntersville. So the arrival of even a small unknown religious group from California did not go by unnoticed.

Shortly after this move, the organization's name was changed to The Church of the Living Light. The Church then acquired a small office building in town for services and classes. In addition, by late 1975 Helen and Brad had purchased an isolated house with acreage on a bluff overlooking Lake Guntersville. Although it was their home, it was also shared with resident students and used for priesthood classes and training. They referred to this house affectionately as "The Casa." At first the town's people were quite friendly and welcoming. In warm response, the Church group reciprocated with open friendship and expressed genuine appreciation for the warm southern hospitality and reception. The Church presented itself as a nondenominational, Christ-based organization and quite openly explained its doctrine and beliefs. Frequent public invitations were extended to the community as a whole to attend open lectures, classes and services. In response, many of the local churches sent individuals or delegations to find out what they were all about.

Before long, the church's belief in past lives and the inclusion of metaphysical, occult, astrological and cabalistic tarot principles and practices in a Christian study program offended the local church and town officials. Church members were branded as "Satan" worshipers. Even after explaining that the word "occult" simply meant concealed or hidden meanings in the Bible or any other sacred text, their fear still led them to consider the group a "cult." Once this happened, doors closed and public fear and suspicion towards the Church and its membership ran rampant. As this hysteria circulated through the area, certain hostile town factions began to systematically harass Helen and Brad in their home by noisily driving through their circular driveway making threatening gestures. In some cases, these groups broke through locked gates and vandalized other parts of the property.

During the move to Guntersville, Brad had his first serious heart attack. He was still recovering in 1975 when all this harassment began. At first he tried to deal with it through the local police and county sheriff's departments. Their lack of response to these acts spoke volumes about the depth and breadth of hostility towards the Church and its membership. On one of the few occasions when a patrol car was actually dispatched to investigate, the officer passed off these incidents as quite harmless. He explained these were just local people wanting to use the driveway to get to a well-established local lovers' rock beside the house overlooking the lake. Apparently the previous owners allowed sightseers and locals access to this area and the policeman said people just hadn't gotten used to not having access. That would have been a plausible explanation had people actually stopped their cars, got out and gone over to the rock, but this never happened.

A few years later the house was vacated and listed for sale with a local broker. When this happened, these earlier events were replaced by more destructive acts. Doors were broken down and windows smashed to gain entry to the house to do extensive interior damage.

Over time, Helen had grown to accept her many physical ailments and conditions as being a part of her transmutation work. She had learned to view them as part of the process of changes in her consciousness as they affected her body. However, within the past two years she had begun to see them as more. In 1975, Helen began studying several books which introduced her to the possibility of creating what she called a "new physical body." She was already familiar with Bible references to building a new spiritual body and about being born again. Commonly accepted interpretations by theologians and Bible scholars referred to these as spiritual transformations rather than physical ones. Through her reading from various sources as well as discussions with the Holy Spirit, more and more she began to see that these obscure scriptural passages did indeed mean an actual physical transformation in matter.

Her personal experience confirmed for her that each time she found, released and transmuted the patterns and restrictions in her own consciousness to death, there were always physical components or aspects of these changes taking place in her body. Being born again in the Spirit of Christ was taking on a new and more practical meaning for her. She began to embrace her previously defined goal of life without death in a different light. Helen saw and experienced this as being a process whereby the Christ, through the Holy Spirit, gradually transformed and transmuted the matter of her natural body (which inevitably dies) into a new physical body. This new body was created from the inside out, so to speak, and actually changed the composition of the physical matter. She believed the new manifestation in matter of this external Christ body was a more perfect vehicle for the expression of the immortal Christ Self and therefore possibly immune to biological death.

In metaphysical writing about evolution, the human Root Race body development is an integral part of the overall evolution of the solar system as it relates to the role of the human kingdom. Each new division of human body development, called a Root Race or Sub-Race body, is first a mutation from, and then a product of, the old or previous one. So in a way, our human bodies are in a constant, although very slow, process of death and rebirth. At the present this happens unconsciously in the matter of human bodies through the gradual gene changes we pass on to our progeny. Helen came to believe that this process can also happen consciously without losing the physical body to death. She received confirmation that this was to be her next commission from God. This new perspective proved not only timely but helpful because energy increased once again bringing more physical crises into Helen's life.

During the four-year period from 1972 to 1976, Helen had five heart attacks, a stroke, and developed hyperglycemia and diabetes. In addition to those conditions, there were times when she went into intermittent comalike states, sometimes lasting for weeks at a time. These were all a result of biological mutations in her body brought on by high levels of creative energy changing her human and body consciousness. During these times, the Holy Spirit was always with her explaining what was happening. It told her that these maladies were normal physical responses to Christ energy breaking down the current restrictions in her body. When the energy reached a kind of biological equilibrium within her, these conditions were then corrected by the Holy Spirit. Having and trusting this information, she did not seek medical treatment for any of these conditions. Instead, she further surrendered to the Christ for healing and regeneration while relying on Ann and others for outer applications of Its healing care.

During a few of these episodes Helen came close to death. In one instance in 1975, she actually went through the process of death, but was sent back. Throughout this event Helen said that she knew she was dying. As she left her body, she moved rapidly towards a series of three ethereal or spiritual gates. She moved easily through the first gate but as she started to pass through the second one, a blazing Being of Light stepped forward and told her that it was not her time to die. He told her that "She must return to Earth to spread purity through her life."

Hearing that she must return to earth and life in her body did not make Helen happy. The years of struggle with her physical health had left her exhausted. However, she knew that she had not completed her spiritual mission and felt that somehow this death experience was a necessary part of her process to fulfill it. So, she returned to her body. From that day on, Helen said that to her, death was reduced to a simple transition from one state of being to another. It no longer held any power over her. She had read accounts of people with no life-threatening disease or fatal injury who just stepped out of their bodies to die. Now she had firsthand knowledge that dying could indeed be that easy.

In July 1976 Helen had another very serious heart attack and once again she came very close to death. She was still recuperating in August when Brad had a series of massive strokes. Needless to say, this put Helen and her staff into considerable crisis. Brad was hospitalized and after a lengthy stay and treatment, came home to convalesce. He was bedridden with severe physical disabilities and mental impairment. He required constant care and companionship, and was lovingly and conscientiously nursed by Ann's husband, Terry, who was also a member of the Church clergy.

Terry very patiently and tenderly made sure he was always secure and comfortable, but eventually it was accepted that Brad needed more physical help than Helen, Ann or Terry could give him. So that fall, Helen took Brad to Denver for physical rehabilitation. Just before they left, Helen asked priesthood member Fred Kipp to be Brad's assistant. In this role and in their absence, Fred was authorized to stand in for Brad as Church president and to chair any necessary board meetings.

Helen and the others took an apartment in Denver to help get them through the period of Brad's rehabilitation therapy. Unfortunately, the damage to his brain and body was more severe than previously thought and the therapy did little to help him recover. Even though Helen was still recovering from her own heart attack, she and Ann did considerable clearance work to aid Brad's healing.

While in Denver, Helen began to experience a sense of relief in being away from the church and all the day-to-day activities in Guntersville. It was during this time that she felt drawn to find a home where she might be secluded not only from the Church but also from the outer world in general. She was told by the Holy Spirit to start looking in the mountains of Colorado. Before long, she discovered a ranch for sale in northwest Colorado near Steamboat Springs that seemed to meet the requirements. However, its price was far beyond their personal means and Brad's condition was far from stable. So, she put off pursuing the ranch until a later time.

Just before Christmas of 1976, Brad started to show improvement. With help, he was able to walk around a little and his mental faculties returned enough for him to communicate better with others. Helen was delighted and encouraged and deeply grateful to God for his improved condition. As she prepared to continue the healing work on him, she was asked by her inner teacher to release Brad to Terry's care and to make a short trip to their Guntersville home. In early January 1977, while she was gone, he suffered a massive heart attack. Shortly after Helen's return to Denver, Brad died.

Brad's death devastated Helen. She loved him dearly and had worked tirelessly towards his healing and recovery. Even though he was never able to fully commit and join her in the depth of her work, he was a strong masculine anchor and support for her as well as a dear and loving husband. The extent of his physical presence and support in Helen's life during this time made much of her spiritual work possible. She now questioned how she could move on without him.

Feeling shattered and vulnerable, Helen's only stability came from her inner guidance and direction. Besides direct contact with the Christ and Holy Spirit, over the years God provided Helen with many inner teachers through numerous Masters, Archangels and Avatars. They all assisted her in the practical day-to-day living and integration of the Christ principles. All worked under the direction of the Christ and with the Holy Spirit in their teaching role with Helen. She continued her scrutiny of all Beings directed to work with her and once satisfied as to their authenticity in the Christ, she faithfully followed their direction without question.

Sometime in 1974, the Master Morya stepped aside as Helen's teacher and the Avatar of Peace took over that role. Up to this point, Morya had been an excellent teacher and friend to Helen, but the nature of changes taking place in Helen's world required a higher level of Being to work with her. (An Avatar is usually a cosmic Being who only descends to the mental plane with a specific divine principle or quality of energy to bring to the planet. From there, they overshadow lesser Avatars who physically embody these new emanations as a living example for humanity.) The cosmic perspective that Peace brought as her teacher profoundly influenced Helen. It expanded her consciousness and inner faculties so that she could more clearly see and understand her next mission in God. Peace was only around for a couple of years while he prepared Helen to meet and work for her next teacher the Avatar of Synthesis. This Avatar worked with Helen for the next twenty years right up to her death. (From this point on, all references to the "Avatar" will mean the Avatar of Synthesis.)

The changes now taking place within her increasingly demanded more and more of her time, energy and focus. She was told by the Avatar that she should begin preparing herself for a more secluded existence, which meant disengaging from public life. This marked the beginning of the end of Helen's teaching life. Since 1968 she had founded a nonprofit church organization, taught individuals and groups, and conducted workshops and conferences on the spiritual principles and techniques she had learned independently and from the Holy Spirit. The Children of Light Society had gone through a reorganization in 1975 and was now officially known as the Church of the Living Light with headquarters in Guntersville. In place and operational was a priesthood of believers and teachers trained and prepared to carry on without her physical day-to-day presence.

Helen was faced with releasing her past in order to more fully embrace her future work. This was not easy for her and she gave herself time to reflect on the task before her. To assist with this transition, she moved into her very own condominium. This move towards privacy helped to create a level of separation from her students as well as to assist in requalifying her life as a single and independent woman. This gave her precious time to herself as well as opportunities to do the things that she truly loved, like once again cooking for herself. Internally, she began to prepare for the eventual separation from the Church. She did not immediately stop teaching though and gave no external signs of her intention or plans. She even may have stepped up her schedule of classes and visited the various church locations more frequently. But, by midyear, it was clear to her that her teaching days were coming to a close.

# Chapter Three

Helen first met Fred Kipp in Los Angeles just a few weeks after Easter in 1974. At the time he was in deep spiritual and psychological crisis. Fred had spent the past eighteen years of his life running from what appeared to be a happy and outwardly conventional childhood. Internally, he was coming to terms with a painfully different perspective.

Before Fred was old enough to attend kindergarten, his mother introduced him to his internal God Self, or the "Magic Presence" as she called It. She spoke to him regularly of a Universal God Presence in a world of Energy, Rays and Ascended Masters who guided humanity and brought the message of God's Light. By the time he was six or seven years old, he was speaking with the Master Saint Germain and accompanying him into the inner realms of spiritual life for instruction at night. Clairvoyantly, Fred was also experiencing and relating to the various spiritual ray energies and the little nature beings all around him. This was his reality, yet he could not speak about it to anyone. His mother had also told him that if he did, he would surely be shunned and ridiculed.

In many respects, his early spiritual experiences were similar to Helen's in that neither could risk openly speaking about them to friends. However, from this point forward, their individual paths took radically different directions. As a teenager, Fred grew to want the comforts of social acceptance and friendship more than he wanted to maintain his internal connection with the God he had known. As a teenager he sought out a new church and religion which might better meet his needs. But this experience left him disenchanted to the point that he questioned the reality of God altogether. He found himself turning his back on his early spiritual experiences in order to seek happiness and fulfillment in an externally oriented life and identity. As part of a continual spiral of spiritual disillusionment, Fred declared himself an atheist in his late twenties.

In 1974, at age thirty, Fred was living "the good life" with his wife and two young daughters in a home in the suburbs with a promising career in banking. Inwardly, however, he was miserable. He found no real meaning or fulfillment in his life and increasingly found it impossible to contain or ignore his clairvoyant sensitivities. His spiritual life and foundation in energy had been too real and compelling for him to abandon. It was while he was in this state of internal desperation that he was introduced to The Children of Light Society. Brought to his knees by the weight of his material life and values, Fred's internal God Self brought him back full circle to God. However, this time, it was his spiritual reality rather than his mother's.

115

In 1975, Fred made the decision to apply for priesthood training. Along with the others, he and his family made the move to Alabama. Their new life turned out to be not the one his wife wanted for herself and, in January 1976, she returned with the children to California, and later that year they divorced.

After his ordination in the Church, Fred was assigned to the Huntsville Parish where he served as co-head, conducting services and teaching classes. It was after Brad's stroke in the fall of 1976 that Fred was asked to be Brad's assistant and stand in for him in his office as president. After Brad's death, Fred temporarily remained in that position, reporting to Helen as spiritual leader of the church. He worked a full-time management job in Huntsville, fulfilled his priesthood duties and responsibilities and continued to attend some of Helen's classes in Guntersville.

One day while Fred was at work, Helen phoned to ask if he had time to look clairvoyantly at something she had stumbled across while doing clearance work on inner planes. (At this point, their relationship was teacher to student or boss to employee as it related to the business affairs of the Church.) Helen gave no clue as to what was going on nor did she in any way try to subtly guide him as he looked in clairvoyantly. What he observed and felt was a marriage celebration all around him. Helen was so strangely silent and contained that he could barely feel her presence on the other end of the phone line. He became petrified as he suddenly realized that what he was watching was an inner marriage ceremony between himself and Helen. Stunned, he had no idea what it meant or its possible implications in his outer life.

After allowing more than sufficient time for him to take it all in, Helen very softly asked him what he saw. Not sure what to do or say, momentarily he thought about telling her that he didn't see anything at all. In a state of shock, extremely fearful of seeming egotistical and arrogant by telling his teacher that he saw himself marrying her, he reported exactly what he saw happening. As he finished, she said "That's what I saw too." Then she asked "Is this something you would like to talk about?" Not knowing exactly why, he said yes and she invited him over to her condominium the next evening.

Over the next few weeks they met several more times to talk about what it would mean if they pursued this inner connection in their outer lives. Each felt a radiant energy of Christ love uniting them together in purpose. Fred felt as though he was being regenerated by the love flowing through him. One night, not being able to deny the experience any longer, Fred told Helen he loved her and surprised himself by asking her to marry him. Apparently she had been going through her own similar experience and immediately said "yes."

A few nights later they were sitting on the sofa talking and Helen told him that God wanted to speak to him through her. He asked Fred if he accepted the sacred trust of the care and keeping of Helen, knowing full well that he only had

Helen through Him and only so long as he was true to the trust. Fred responded that he did.

Afterward, Helen explained to Fred that God had spoken to her earlier that day. He told her that the New Body work ahead of her was going to be extremely difficult. Further, she was unsure if it was possible to complete the entire work in this embodiment. There was a lot involved in the process and even though initiated by the Christ Energy, there was considerable opposition to it in physical matter and on the inner, spiritual realms. This was because the very nature of matter, as well as the orientation of many inner beings, is to resist attempts to change the evolutionary pace of creation.

Helen said that she had already made the commitment to God and agreed to follow through with the work no matter what opposition she met or how long it took. God told her it was likely that her consciousness would spend considerable time out of her physical body on inner planes while her physical body went through drastic change. He told her that it was Fred who would be her "solid rock," or physical anchor, to connect her to the physical plane while this all went on. Without this anchor, it was clear she could not go on. Further, she told Fred that their life together would likely be difficult, lonely and without public support.

Subsequently, during their lengthy discussions about marriage, Helen was very direct and honest with Fred about the severity of her life and spiritual work. As completely as she could at the time, she explained her New Body work to him. Although he had been a priest in the church for a few years and thought he understood what building a new physical body meant, he found that he really knew very little. In the Church most people spoke of Helen's work as physical perfection or as immortality.

But Helen rejected those kinds of references. She said that in all life, perfection is an illusion. Anything perfect today becomes imperfect tomorrow as newer or better ways of doing something emerge. So, too, with the human physical body. Human perception of physical perfection changes with evolution. The body gradually mutates and changes its form and internal functions to support human life as environmental conditions change. As far as immortality goes, she said we are already immortal human spirits who for a time take on physical form in order to participate in and experience God's creative process in dense physical matter.

She went on to say that even if she was successful in building a new physical body and for a time did not die, human evolution would eventually catch up, rendering the New Body she was building today simply the natural one of the future. At that point, once again she would be subject to the same life and death cycles as all humans in that level of physical matter. If it was her job again, she would create a newer body that would once again be immune to death for a time.

To her, this process would repeat itself until all of the human Root Race bodies in this earth period are a reality on the physical plane. When the last body had been raised to a certain point in its spiritual evolution then humankind and the world would be Christed and ready to begin a new creative process in the "Father" energy of God.

As Helen assessed this New Body work, she promised God that she would always rely on the Christ and Holy Spirit for her health and well-being. To do this she had to turn her back completely on conventional human wisdom and the medical ways of the world and put her life totally in God's hands. With this surrender, God assured her that all the physical and spiritual resources needed for her life and work would be supplied to her. For Helen, this commitment from God was essential. Relying on it completely was the only way she could cope with the immensity of her task. From her perspective, many of the physical ailments and symptoms that doctors routinely treat as curable (or to return the body to normal health) are the very physical mutations or transition changes necessary to eventually break down the natural body in order to create a new one.

Because of the nature of Helen's life and the extreme conditions of her work and commitment to God, it was necessary for her to approach her marriage with Fred in a contractual, businesslike manner. In their life together it was essential that Fred understand, accept and agree unconditionally to support Helen's spiritual life as the center of their relationship.

There were a few additional requests Helen asked of Fred as part of their marriage agreement. First and foremost, she asked him to give her the personal freedom to follow God's directions without question, challenge or interference by him. In essence, to give her the freedom to be at all times, which included supporting her independent right to live or die based on her own relationship with God, not his. She asked him never to take her to a doctor or a hospital. She said that if she ever went into a hospital she would not come out alive. Also, she asked him never to allow people into their home during deep and difficult cycles of her work. This was because she didn't think she could survive the emotional reaction in the matter of others' bodies to the level of creative energy working in her body.

Fred agreed to all of her requests. He did so as fully and as consciously aware of their personal consequences as a person can be without knowing what to expect from actual experience. This set the foundation for their relationship. They had nowhere to turn other than to God for the help, strength and the resources to do what was needed in their life to support Helen's mission in God. With that trust as the basis for their marriage relationship and spiritual work together, they were married on October 8, 1977.

That was a special day for both of them. But it was especially significant for Fred because Helen's son, Jeffery, officially came into his life. From the first day they met there was a deep connection made. It was more like a reunion of long-lost friends than two people meeting for the first time. There was something about Jeffery's very being that reached out and touched Fred's heart and Jeffery seemed to embrace Fred with considerable love. Both Helen and Fred were overwhelmed by Jeffery's apparent immediate and genuine acceptance of him as his mother's new husband.

Their relationship only got closer and stronger. For Fred, Jeffery was truly his son and eventually Jeffery embraced Fred as his stepfather. From Helen's viewpoint, it seemed Jeffery got along better with Fred than with her. Their estrangement over the years had taken its toll on their relationship. Helen always felt that he did not know how to be free and easy with her. This is something she dearly wanted but could never seem to have.

As the years passed, Fred became a kind of bridge between the two of them. Although there were times when Helen and Jeffery could deeply communicate with each other, it seemed to Helen that Jeffery was more comfortable having Fred serve as an intermediary. Because of his love for them both, Fred gladly played this role in the hopes that one day Jeffery could come to Helen directly.

# Chapter Four

In preparation for their new life together as well as to support Helen's increasing needs for seclusion, changes were gradually implemented in the church structure and operations. In his role of managing church business, Fred had been working on ways to foster a greater independence among priests and members. Over the years, people had grown very attached to Helen as their spiritual leader which often stood in the way of internalizing the very principles and practices she taught and lived. He worked at restructuring activity towards a more practical orientation to encourage individuals as well as church officers to rely more on their own internal authority and connection with God. This was an uphill path that could be taken only in incremental steps.

After the wedding, Helen and Fred moved out of the Casa in Guntersville into a small condominium they purchased in Steamboat Springs, Colorado. This was to be their temporary home to live and work in by themselves, away from the activity of church life and the presence of students in their home. About 165 miles northwest of Denver, Steamboat Springs is a rural mountain ranching community near which a ski resort has been built.

Even though Helen and Fred knew each other on inner planes and from their church interaction, they still had much to learn about one another in their daily life. Helen also needed time alone to begin to separate from the public demands of her previous household, her present students and the church. For Fred, this time was an opportunity for him to adjust to his new relationship with Helen and to become conscious of his inherent sense of masculine superiority with women. He had some internalization and transmutation work of his own to do in fulfilling his agreements with Helen. Releasing his foundation and patterns of masculine conditioning was essential if he was to be able to give Helen the freedom of being he had promised.

Although Fred faced challenges in his life with Helen, he never felt more loved by anyone in the world. With her love came the freedom for him to be what and who he was without fear of being controlled, condemned, criticized or judged by her. When speaking as his spiritual teacher, she never told him what he needed to do or demand that he change. She always presented possible consequences of his thoughts, feelings and actions. Then, without requirement that he accept her guidance, she suggested initiatory courses of action to get the most transmutation out of any situation. Her love was long-suffering and remained constant in the face of his considerable attempts to control her self-expression and life. When he finally began the process of facing himself and saw just how manipulating and controlling he had been towards her, it was difficult for Fred to believe that Helen could still love him. But she did! No matter what was going on within him, Fred could always feel the strength and support of her love all around him. Always, it was a tangible presence and foundation upon which his personality transformation was anchored and possible.

Fred was somewhat experienced with the inner life and had done clearance for several years, but he was not prepared for the intensity with which Helen approached these realities. This included the clearance process. What she needed to know for her life and work came directly from the inner planes. This information needed to be deciphered through intuitive reasoning, clear thinking, and applied as if her life depended on it. In point of fact to her, it did. When she surrendered to the body-building process, she turned everything over to God.

This was frightening to Fred because often she was relying on his inner faculties for the information she needed to determine what to do next. Initially, his ego soared in self-importance, but in no time he felt an incredible weight of responsibility that brought him back down to reality. Eventually this shattered his ego sufficiently for the Holy Spirit and the Avatar to prepare him to allow the Christ energy to carry the weight of his burden. He began to realize that what they were involved in was serious business and that he was not fully up to the task yet. Life in Steamboat Springs was a very difficult transition period for Helen as well. With all the inner work necessary to support Helen's body process, setting up and managing a house on their own proved harder than expected. Therefore it was decided that additional help was needed in their lives. So, someone from Helen's previous home staff as well as Ann and Terry moved in to assist with their clearance and domestic needs.

At this time, Helen was learning how to allow the Christ energy to change the matter of her physical body without dying. She already knew and experienced her immortal God Self apart from her body, but God wanted her to learn how to bring that immortal Spirit into her physical body so that it could be transformed into a new one. As always, when faced with tasks from God she felt unprepared for what was ahead. From experience, though, she knew that if this new body was possible, God's energy and not her own would ultimately get the job done.

Even though there were a few books in publication that alluded to or glamorized this possibility, the Avatar told her that no human had ever accomplished this at the dense physical level that would be worked out in her body. He reemphasized also that it was an extremely dangerous process because evolutionary matter is not programmed to yield to accelerated DNA change. Therefore, she should be absolutely certain that she was willing to risk her life in matter to advance the New Body development process. He warned her further that the physical intensity of creative energy working on her body would have drastic (and possibly dangerous) physical effects on those around her. As a result it would affect people psychologically, leading to misunderstanding and distorted perceptions of her spiritual teaching, life and work.

As Helen learned more about the realities of this process, she realized that even though her students were initiates and genuinely wanted to learn from her, they did not have the same commitment or faith to sacrifice at the level necessary to participate with her in the process. This was not a criticism of their spiritual commitment, their faith or their individual relationship with God, but simply a matter of fact to Helen. She had already experienced alarming distortions and misunderstandings in her students to what she had previously taught and the Avatar told her it would only get worse.

In addition, the unconscious psychic reactions and projections from the collective student entity made her feel alienated and estranged from the group she had taught for almost ten years. Her students were working as hard as they could but she had a big head start in transmuting and changing her consciousness, body and life. Presently, rather than the gap closing between her and her students, it was widening. Helen just didn't have the energy to work on herself and to keep her students working on themselves at the same time. In addition, although many believed building a new physical body was possible intellectually or spiritually, most had considerable difficulty accepting it physically.

Helen agonized over the student situation for the first half of 1978. Her love for all left her feeling unable to separate from them. Repeatedly, the Holy Spirit had told her that in her heart she was too generous to people whom she loved which worked to her own detriment. Often to block the unconscious attempts from others to control or restrict her energy activities, she had to act decisively and dispassionately which made her appear ruthless. At times, her lack of emotional support and sympathy for her family, friends and students must have seemed emotionally cold and uncaring. This was far from the truth - she was always just way ahead of her time in her ability to love from a higher place of purpose and spiritual holding.

In mid-1978, the Avatar asked Helen to resign as the spiritual leader of the Church. She was told that no amount of explanation would satisfy the priesthood or membership. Therefore, He suggested she simply state that she was resigning for "irreconcilable differences." In the meantime, Fred was to remain on as head of the Church until that transition was complete. The Avatar also asked Helen to establish a retreat home for those people sent her way by God to go through similar physical body changes. He stated that a protected environment away from the prevailing demands, responsibilities and dangers of worldly life was absolutely essential to surviving the process.

Helen now questioned where the best location might be for her new phase of work. Geographically, Steamboat Springs is nestled in the middle of the Rocky

Mountains and is isolated from the rest of Colorado, not to mention the rest of the country.  Just getting to the area by car during the winter months was tedious at best.  Often the weather was so bad that shuttle flights from Denver were frequently delayed if not canceled altogether.  The ranch Helen was considering, with its elevation and surrounding National Forest wilderness, was remote even from the town of Steamboat Springs.  After living in the area during a hard winter, Helen decided that what she needed was seclusion, not isolation.  After this realization, the Avatar suggested she look in Colorado Springs for a new home.

# Chapter Five

Helen resigned her position as spiritual leader of the Church of the Living Light in August 1978. This sent shock waves through the organization and was an extremely difficult transition for everyone involved. Fred continued on with his position and responsibilities in the church with Helen's support. This was hard on Helen at many levels, but by this point in her life, she had developed the discipline and will to move forward when it was necessary. However, moving ahead without outer structure is never easy.

Often there is a misconception of the differences between religious and spiritual work. Usually, religious work involves an outer world structure with an established foundation and order in which its activities take place and have meaning. Spiritual work, in contrast, often involves an absence of outer form and revolves around an ideal or inner principle struggling for external expression and acceptance. Although Helen never discounted the distinct possibility of immediate manifestation of anything where God was concerned, she realized that all aspects of material form originated in the cosmic realm of ideas. Ideas take time to work their way through the various levels of the cosmic dimensions until they become an objective reality. If there was ever any doubt about that, all she had to do was to look at the evolutionary world around her.

To Helen, every new spiritual movement or religion started out as a divinely inspired idea. This idea took time to be defined and considerable effort to be communicated to people sufficiently for them to understand and embrace. As this happened, the idea became differentiated or made practical in matter and took on material existence in the lives of people around the world. More often than not, in their infancy, most new religious movements met considerable opposition and people risked their lives to make their spiritual message known to the world.

This was the nature of Helen's spiritual work. Every task she was given by God required a considerable amount of inner-directed alignment and focus. This happened through practical definition, prayer and hard work just to bring the basic energy principles down through the planes to a point where they could be expressed in language.

Helen always approached any spiritual task impersonally knowing that her role in it might very well be to work on some detail of a greater pattern or plan on inner planes for physical manifestation. She accepted that, at some point, what she contributed to the process might be passed off to other people along the line, for further work, before it ultimately made its way into physical reality. This acceptance required that she maintain a position of personal neutrality, without attachments to the various aspects and cycles of her work. At the outset, she never knew for certain where she fit into the overall scheme and whether she would ever physically see the results of her work. This factor contributed to her incredible faith and trust in God.

However, this did not stop her from proceeding in an organized fashion as if the desired results would happen in a few years. Her whole life was a creative experiment in what is possible in God. She used every activity in her life to contact higher creative energy and to learn how to make it practical. Everything she did in her home, work and life was qualified in this way. For Helen, everything around her worked as a magnet to attract and anchor higher levels of Christ energy for external expression in physical life. It was with this orientation that she approached her activities to create a retreat home.

By the fall of 1978, Helen and Fred purchased a home in Colorado Springs, Colorado. This was to be the new home of Helen and Fred, Ann and her husband Terry, and another student couple, Jef and Julie. It was a large, Tudor-style house with several acres of grounds in the Broadmoor area of Colorado Springs. Although the exterior of the house had the stately appearance of an old English country home, the inside looked as if it hadn't been redone since the early 1950s. With its thick plaster walls and heavy wood beams, it emanated stability and protection. It was the perfect house for Helen to transform and a fantastic creative project to draw energy for a retreat home. Helen envisioned that this would be a protected and secluded environment for her to further her New Body work. They purchased this house entirely on faith. They had used almost all of their available resources to buy the house and had no idea how they could afford the mortgage payments and its upkeep, let alone the remodeling necessary to make it livable. In addition, the house in Guntersville had been on the market for a while and had not sold. Maintaining this property added to their expenses.

One particular feature of this house that Helen dearly loved was a large library extending partially over the drive through the entrance portico below. She used this as her office and as a classroom to teach household classes. This was a magnificent room with spectacular views of Cheyenne Mountain. Somehow, while in this room, time was meaningless and she could just be. It was probably the only place in the house where Helen had any peace away from the remodeling work. More importantly, it gave her refuge from the constant swirl of emotional reactive energy and pressure from Fred and the others in the household. Often this centered on the heavy financial and physical burdens the house represented. Eventually this pressure escalated to a point which forced a breakup of the other two couples. This left Fred, Ann and Jef to continue with Helen in the work.

By this time, Helen's relationship with her son Jeffery was closer and much improved. In the past year he had visited Helen and Fred several times and was now attending college in Tennessee. In early 1979, Helen and Fred traveled to Tennessee to visit him at school. Prior to their visit, they were informed that Jeff's Uncle Glenn was seriously ill and hospitalized for treatment of cancer. Before returning home, they visited him in the hospital.

Considering Glenn's medical condition and his debilitating treatments, he was quite warm and friendly towards them both. He was very weak and asked Helen to sit on his bed. Gently, he took her hand and said quite clearly and distinctly "Helen, I was wrong about you and I am sorry." From what Helen had spoken about her history and relationship with Glenn, Fred never thought a reconciliation possible between them. However, in his life with Helen he had learned never to underestimate the power of God to arrange or resolve circumstances and events. On their drive to the airport after the visit, Fred asked Helen if she thought Glenn would also tell Jeffery about how wrong he had been about her. She replied, "It is enough for me that Glenn had the courage to tell me. I trust that God will work out the rest with Jeffery." A few months later, they heard he had died.

In early 1980, Helen asked Fred how he felt about selling the Colorado Springs house. This came as quite a surprise since they had just come through a grueling two-year period of renovation, remodeling and redecoration. Although not finished, the house was beginning to feel warm and to look elegant. Each room was charged with Light and protection and Its radiant beauty was beginning to show more each day. But for as much as Helen loved the house and valued its protected seclusion, she was prepared to walk away from it if needed. She explained to Fred that the Avatar had recently discussed with her that the house was only the preparation and training stage for establishing a retreat home. He said the actual retreat would not manifest physically for some years and its location was to be in Australia. Furthermore, he suggested that they sell the house and travel to Australia to find where the retreat would eventually be located. This trip was needed to physically release and anchor Helen's retreat energy and work to date. The Avatar also told Helen that sometime in the near future they would relocate to Australia probably for a period of about ten years.

Although not directly told so by the Avatar, intuitively Helen knew that when she moved to Australia her life would become increasingly more secluded. When she had completed her New Body, she suspected she would once again return to the outer world. At the end of a ten-year period, she fully expected the New Body to be the shining physical example of God's creative power to transform matter on the physical plane. This was the "Light Image" at the end of the New Body tunnel and her gift from God to help see her through the process.

She embraced and nourished this image within herself at all times and held It firmly within her heart and consciousness.

The house was sold and by early March 1980, Helen, Fred and Ann were booked for a six-week trip to Australia. (Jef remained in Colorado Springs.) For most of the trip, Helen was physically active and enjoyed touring, but she did not feel very well and the travel was very rough on her. The physical changes taking place at this time seemed to accelerate as she crossed the equator and headed into the southern hemisphere. She often said that had she known just how poorly she was going to feel all the time, she might have opted out of it in the earlier stages. As they arrived at the last destination on their trip, Helen suddenly lost all physical vitality and had to spend much of the time in bed.

On one of the days when Helen was able to get out and drive around, they stumbled upon a mountainous area above the Gold Coast of Queensland that seemed almost ethereal. Intuitively, Helen knew that she was at last closing in on the spot to which the Avatar was leading her. Within a few days, they found the spot on a farm property for sale. The retreat energy Helen had been planning and holding for, finally released from inner planes through her body into the earth. For the next several days after this event, Helen was in a very weakened and fragile physical state while her body recovered from the effects of having so much energy pour through her. Once her vitality returned, she was told that nothing more was needed there and that after returning home they were to prepare to relocate to Australia within a few years.

During their trip back to the states, Helen passed a point of no return in her work. Even though she had previously felt the painful effects of the energy quite physically, the work had primarily taken place within her subtle, inner bodies. This was preparation work necessary to create a new Light Pattern Body in etheric matter to be impressed upon her dense physical body during the next phase of the work. In order for this impression to be made, her body's natural defense or autoimmune system had to be broken down. This was necessary so that it did not attack and destroy the fragile physical effects of the New Body Light Pattern as it crossed the bridge to the physical plane. When this was in place, this Light Body would sustain Helen's life and bodily functions while it began the long process of changing the cellular DNA codes. This process would create the New Body from the inside out. However, once her organs and systems began this change, they would no longer support her natural body functions and therefore her life. Her only path of physical survival was moving forward with the energy work.

Through clearance, Helen discovered that, contained within the underlying energy pattern of the natural body's cellular structure, are latent biological triggering mechanisms. These are activated to break down the body only when certain evolutionary conditions or creative energy purposes are met. These are defense mechanisms to prevent premature transition mutations to the next level of evolutionary human body. As modern science has discovered, certain chemical concentrations or nuclear energy overwhelm these DNA defense mechanisms and physical mutation rapidly occurs. This same principle applies to potent levels of spiritual creative energies as well.

Apparently, in Australia, the release of the retreat energy through her body in conjunction with the energy field reversal of the southern hemisphere, activated these breakdown triggers. The last latent trigger was activated on the return trip when she crossed the equator and reentered the forcefield of the northern hemisphere. This initiated the next phase of dense physical adjustments and mutations of the New Body process.

After returning from Australia, Helen and Fred spent the summer of 1980 at their Guntersville home. The house had been on the market for some time without results, and the purpose for this stay was to make improvements to enhance its sale potential. In August, they traveled to Tennessee for the marriage of her son. Jeffery and Brenda had been high-school sweethearts, and according to Helen, Brenda was the loving and supportive partner that she always hoped Jeffery would find. Helen genuinely loved Brenda and was delighted that Jeffery was settling into his own adult life with her.

In October, Helen and Fred returned to Colorado Springs and remained there for six months. From here on, the work progressed to the point of constant energy attacks to break down the cellular structure of her natural body. As part of the process, the innate energy of the natural world turned on her. The friendly beings of the elements she knew and loved as a child became unfriendly and menacing. This was because they were older versions of the Holy Spirit energy, naturally flowing through the earth and her instinctive human body. The new human body she was building would be of a new order and vibration of Christ Holy Spirit energy. Presently, this energy is alien to the matter and consciousness of this dense, earthly realm.

The earth no longer felt like home to Helen. It became a hostile environment with lower earth beings challenging the biological changes in her life. They threatened her physical life everywhere she turned. She was told that unfortunately these conditions would continue until the New Body was complete and was functional in dense physical matter. This was to be the reality and condition of her life, so she needed to accept it and move on. The only alternative at this point was to leave the process and the physical plane (through death) because there was no going back. She was also told that from now on she would find no written material in the world to guide her. She was stepping into uncharted territory and would have to rely entirely on her inner guidance and learn as she went along.

In September 1980, two years after Helen's resignation from the Church, the Avatar advised Helen that it was time for Fred to resign as president of the Church. Fred needed to devote all of his time and energy to support Helen in the difficult body work ahead. This was a big load removed from them both, but especially so for Fred. He felt pulled in two directions by his attempts to lead the Church at a distance and support Helen's work - and it hadn't worked very well. From this time forward, other than a few exceptions, no one (other than those immediately around her) had direct contact with Helen. The following year, Helen invited two of her former students to visit, asking them to be points of contact for any future inquiries or communication from former students who might desire to reach her. Having these intermediaries gave Helen the protection she needed to continue her work.

By early spring of 1981, Helen and Fred moved to Breckenridge, Colorado. (Ann remained in Colorado Springs with Jef.) The reason for this move was that the Avatar told Helen the next phase of the work would be easier in high-altitude conditions. This was a very difficult time for Helen as she spent most of the time in bed in a semi-comalike state. At first Fred was quite frightened by her condition but later learned that this experience of caring for her was essential for him to learn how to more deeply trust the Avatar and the Christ energy stream working on Helen.

Among the many beneficial events of the Breckenridge period was that Helen and Fred were directed to the hot springs pool in Glenwood Springs, Colorado. When Helen was able, they soaked in this pool once a week. With each visit, clearance revealed that the Christ used the physical mineral properties in the water to begin making adjustments in Helen's body chemistry. Sometimes higher energy needs a material catalyst or host to work through, and for this phase of body work, the minerals in the water were just what were needed. These weekly hot springs visits also helped to incrementally change the chemical balance in Fred's body as well. This was necessary so that his physical body did not go into shock by being around Helen with the changes taking place in her. Helen and Fred continued to use the hot springs twice yearly for the next twelve years.

Four months after their arrival in Breckenridge, the Avatar announced to Helen that she would not be returning to Australia anytime soon. This was a shock to them both! Everything they had done for the past year and a half had been in preparation for a move to Australia. (Being guided from inner planes is obviously not an exact science. Constant adjustments and changes in perspective occur just as they do for humans trying to negotiate life and direction on the physical plane.) After this startling information, Helen and Fred felt bounced around by the changing instructions from the Avatar as well as shifts in the energy patterns sustaining their life. It was not until much later that they realized that this chaotic period prepared them to further surrender to life in the constant, ever-changing flow of energy and change. They had to become comfortable and functional with the chaos and to learn to trust God at increasingly higher levels. Although they might not be able to see a purpose in what was happening at any given time, staying aligned to their energy direction was their only hope of survival in what was ahead of them.

Later that year, Helen and Fred visited Jeffery and Brenda in their newly purchased home in Medina, Tennessee. It was during this visit that Helen began to experience severe physical difficulties. After viewing the situation clairvoyantly, it was revealed that the earth energy of that area seemed to be attacking her natural body. Their first inclination was to return immediately to Colorado, but the Avatar very forcefully intervened and told Helen that what was happening was exactly what she needed and that in fact, it had been planned to happen.

He further explained that besides the genetic markers known to science, each human born into a body takes on the regional evolutionary matter and consciousness of the area on earth into which they are born. Along with genetic body characteristics, this matter is the karmic energy foundation of the human physical body which is needed for human growth in consciousness in any given lifetime. This matter contains within it the evolutionary energy records of previous Root Race bodies. It represents the individual and collective karmic challenges or limitations to be balanced or worked out by applying human consciousness to the life experiences in that body. Often in old age or when people begin to die they feel drawn back to the area of their birth because this is truly their home in matter. Helen was told that this earth force energy working to reclaim the regional energy of her natural body could be used to speed up greatly the breakdown process of her natural body.

Finding out that Helen needed to return to the place of her birth was a real turning point. It was explained that out of necessity, in building the New Body, she would have to live near her birthplace in Tennessee. She would have to remain there until the earth force energy of the area had done its job of reclaiming her natural body and until the New Body had grown to replace the departing natural one. The one positive aspect of this news was that finally Helen would be physically close to her son Jeffery. Hopefully this would help to complete the healing process from his estrangement from her. She was also eager to build a new and closer adult relationship with him and Brenda. Encouraged by the fact that the Avatar told Helen this was the last and most critical part of the New Body process, Helen and Fred and Ann moved to Jackson, Tennessee in early October 1981.

# PART SIX:

# SYNTHESIS

*Frederick R. Kipp*

# Chapter One

The countryside and farmland around Jackson, Tennessee, is quite beautiful with gently rolling hills and numerous fields of cotton, soybeans and corn. Located between Nashville, 125 miles to the east and Memphis, 85 miles to the west, it is well situated to access both cities. It was an ideal location for Helen's energy work, near Jeffery and Brenda and the Medina area where she grew up.

As Helen, Fred and Ann settled into life in Jackson, they had to make many significant adjustments. They no longer had an external focus in the world by which their lives were anchored. The Church, with its structures and members, was gone from their lives as well as the task of creating the retreat home. To Helen this was a relief, enabling her to move further into the seclusion necessary for her work. But for Fred and Ann, this was a considerable challenge. Their orientation and purpose was to support Helen's work through the practical elements of living as well as providing the energy protections around her. This focus was the training ground for their own personal transmutation.

Many people talk about the appeal of a secluded life with the freedom to focus on the inner realms and their own spiritual growth and identity. But probably few understand the challenges this brings in confronting the cultural patterns and conditioning of a lifetime which attribute identity and purpose with external productivity and outer world activity. First and foremost for Fred and Ann was the challenge of meeting and interacting with others. They no longer had an easily recognizable form of work or explanation for their life. Having no church affiliation or organization to refer to, they could no longer state they were clergy. How did they explain what they did without eliciting instantaneous reactions? With Helen's New Body work now their main focus, suddenly their life and activities went well beyond the comprehension and acceptance of those who lived around them. It took constant vigilance to create and maintain an outer form and appearance in their life that was sufficient or acceptable.

This was especially true in relation to Jeffery, Brenda and Helen's parents and sisters. Their life was not what it appeared from the outside. Even though no one directly asked, they probably had many questions about what Helen and Fred did everyday and how they financially supported themselves. Helen, Fred and Ann did what they could to veil the reality of their life's spiritual essence, purpose and nature. This was necessary to provide the needed protection for Helen. She was moving into very dangerous and uncharted areas of spiritual energy with its effects on the dense physical body. There was nothing in the external world to sanction this work, let alone support it. It was difficult at best, and up to Helen to lead Fred and Ann through the demands and chaos of this transition to the stark realities of an inner life existence. Helen's deep and sustaining relationship with the Christ and Holy Spirit along with her guidance from the Avatar were their only stable foundation.

Everything that happened in their daily life depended on the work going on in Helen's body. Often this was grueling with little time off. Energy work went on twenty-four hours a day, seven days a week and often Helen needed the most clearance work during the middle of the night. Sometimes, for months on end, Helen reversed her schedule to be up during the night and sleep during the day. There were breaks, though, after a plateau of energy work had been reached. During these times Helen was quite active and made up for lost time in doing the things she wanted to do before the next level and phase of body work began again.

Both Fred and Ann were strongly affected by the energy working on Helen. Even though they had lived with her previously, those experiences were tame compared to the work that began in Jackson. The intensified levels of energy now working on her body, caused greater shock and trauma in their systems and bodies. There were new levels of psychological patterns and physical barriers that surfaced, challenging their belief in their ability to cope. These unconscious obstacles needed definition and attention which led to the necessity for making adjustments. These experiences and their resolution by the Christ taught each of them more about breaking patterns and limitations in their own consciousness and bodies to keep them transmuting. Both were determined to make the necessary changes to continue contributing to the work.

However, Helen's very life, which she had committed for the work to move forward, was at stake. There is a huge difference between contribution and commitment. To illustrate the difference, Helen often used a well-known little breakfast saying: "In relation to a breakfast of bacon and eggs, the chicken contributes but the pig is committed!" Literally, Helen had to carry the load of making a new life in Jackson and establishing the daily activities for the energy work.

In the beginning, Fred and Ann grumbled constantly about all the changes they had to make and the personal desires and comforts they had to sacrifice. A few months after arriving in Jackson, Helen reached the limits of her tolerance of their negative attitude. Stressed by the painful energy activity in her body, she told them that she would give anything to be around people whose orientation was to celebrate Spirit rather than complaining about all the changes they had to make. Both Ann and Fred were stunned! They had each seen themselves as totally in support of God's work through Helen.

Helen suggested that they start going to local Pentecostal church meetings to learn how to truly and joyfully surrender to the Holy Spirit. This seemed to lift the burden of responsibility of their struggle to surrender off of Helen. After a few years of public witness for the Spirit of God in their lives, they were finally able to join Helen in celebrating what God was doing in her body and life as well as in their own.

Helen, Fred and Ann frequently traveled, taking trips across the country for clearance work. These were working trips planned and directed by the Holy Spirit and the Avatar to many of the power points on the earth. At these locations, spiritual powers of the past had worked miracles through nature for those who believed and surrendered to their energies. However, over time the spiritual energy flowing through many of these points had been misused and corrupted leaving negative residual effects that are no longer constructive at this point in planetary evolution. These are dangerous points that can work malevolently on those who visit them and are openings for this distorted energy to pass into and express through humanity.

From time to time, Helen was asked to physically visit these spots or areas to be the physical contact point for the Christ to reclaim the old energy records (both positive and negative), and the nature beings of the earth still caught up in them. In addition, the energy of the Christ replaced the existing energy structures with new ones to support Its creative mission on Earth. The work that took place at these points simultaneously worked on Helen's body. Sometimes she was directed to places that needed a new energy structure where none existed before. After doing this work, the Holy Spirit revealed to Helen that these new structures were necessary to help change the planetary energy polarity to be receptive for higher energies seeking manifestation on Earth.

These were not easy trips for Helen, often leaving her physical body in a weakened state. Sometimes they would spend additional days or a week in the area just to get Helen to the point where she could travel home. Upon returning home, it might take her several more weeks or months to recover. Although not always immediately apparent, everything Helen was asked to do by the Christ or Avatar had positive benefits for her life and work. Knowing this made it easier each time to make the trips and face their inherent adversities.

The instruction for most of these trips came with little notice and usually at inconvenient times and with little financial resources available. Often, she would get up in the morning and without warning tell Fred and Ann to start packing to leave for somewhere later that day or the next day. Sometimes their travel was solely for energy work on Helen's body. These trips were scheduled according to energy cycles or releases (such as the solstices and equinoxes) to bring about certain physical changes in her body at appropriate or recurring times each year. The trips to the Colorado hot mineral waters were designed to use existing physical energy sources as a vehicle to work on her body. These trips and others like them became routine and therapeutic in nature, just like a patient going for intense medical treatments. The side effects often were remarkably similar, as was the recovery time needed to regain strength and vitality.

Occasionally, the Avatar directed Helen to visit various people so that her physical presence could be used to transfer particular energies they needed in their life and work. In 1978, she was asked to visit a well-known and elderly astrologer, who lived near San Francisco. When Helen pressed the Avatar for information as to why, he said only that she had something this man needed from her. Despite little information on the purpose of the visit, the astrologer scheduled an appointment for them in August at his home.

By the time Helen and Fred arrived, they still had little to tell him about why they had traveled from Colorado to sit almost silently in his living room. After some minor pleasantries and refreshments, he asked Helen why she had come. Very honestly, Helen replied that her teacher had sent her, only telling her that she had something he needed but she did not know what. To say the least, this was a very tense and difficult situation for all.

He seemed mildly amused and at one point appeared on the verge of asking Helen more questions. However, rather than doing so he seemed to be lifted up in consciousness and said very little from that point on. After a very awkward and silent few minutes, he said he was tired and needed to rest. It was only after the visit that the Avatar offered any kind of explanation. He told Helen that through his astrological work and writings, this man was also involved in New Body work. The Avatar went on to say that due to his advanced age and present physical condition, he had taken his work as far as he could go in this embodiment. However, his work was significant and he deserved to have energy contact through Helen and with the work on her body so it could be recorded in his bodies for continuing work in his next embodiment. Since consciously he was unaware of his role in the work, his potential reaction to hearing the reason for the visit might have deflected the energy released to him.

Almost immediately after arriving in Jackson, Helen's hope of a renewed relationship with Jeffery seemed to erode. It became clear that he needed time to release his pain and to heal the emotional wounds from his sense of abandonment by her. Although they had reconciled somewhat during their previous visits, reentering his life in Tennessee after all these years was another matter altogether. Helen understood his situation and lovingly gave him plenty of room to vent his feelings towards her. Generally she did this without defense of herself or her prior actions. Although prepared for his reaction, at first she was overwhelmed by the force of his anger towards her. To help resolve the situation, Helen and Fred silently prayed and did clearance work to handle their part. She believed that someday he would be able to understand the nature of her relationship with God and why it had been necessary for them to part. Within a year, relations with Jeffery improved considerably and he seemed happier about his mother living nearby.

One of Helen's true joys was listening to Jeffery sing solos in his church. After each performance and for days afterward, Helen basked in the spirit of the Christ that flowed through Jeffery's voice. She said that from the moment Jeffery stood up to sing, the Holy Spirit filled the church. And that through his voice, It anointed all present with the Light and Love of the Christ. She never felt closer to him than when she joined him in his enormous love of God and was lifted up in joyful celebration through his songs of praise.

# Chapter Two

During the winter of 1982, one of the first things the Avatar had Helen do was to walk daily through the hilly woodlands of a local park in Jackson. Physically, the purpose of these walks was to expose her body to the area earth force energy. The whole reason for living in Jackson was for that purpose, and the sooner she got started the better. Winter was a good time for Helen to do this kind of activity because the full force of the nature energy is withdrawn into the earth for regeneration before it reemerges in the spring. The Avatar wanted her exposed to this earth energy, not devastated by it.

Routinely, Helen, Fred and Ann walked on a prescribed path through the woods. Many times it would take hours to make the circuit and more hours of recovery and clearance to deal with the breakdown effects in Helen. By that spring, the process of local matter invading her body was set so automatically in place that these walks were no longer necessary.

To replace the walks, the Avatar asked Helen to make daily outings in the area. This began the next stage of breakdown work by expanding Helen's contact with the area and people around her. At first, this meant driving around West Tennessee to reacquaint herself with the vicinity. As they toured the places where she had lived as a child, she spoke to Fred and Ann about her early life there to help release the memory records deeply locked in the matter of her physical body. Previously, she had done this in her mental, emotional and etheric double bodies but there is a component of the collective cultural conditioning and personal experience that also registers itself in the physical body. These psychic records in dense matter are the hardest to release and transmute.

This was important. Rather than just recreating old psychically charged experiences or traumatic memories, she allowed them to release. If she relived them in the present as they were experienced and recorded, even for a moment, the psychic energy would lock down her physical organs and systems thereby threatening her life and interfering with the inner work. Through this process, she thoroughly forgave herself and all involved for being young, unconscious and inexperienced. Helen surrendered to the Christ to transmute the experiences through her new perspectives and understanding of the role they played in her life.

Helen left nothing to chance and every week methodically covered more and more of the physical areas of her childhood. She followed the Avatar's directions to the letter. On one of these weekly outings, she retraced her marriage trip with Ferrell to Corinth, Mississippi. On another, they drove to the

Tennessee River and to the cabin area where she, Ferrell and his brother and wife went for fishing weekends. She even toured the areas where her sisters and husbands had lived as adults, as well as the birthplaces of her father and mother.

In addition to these trips, Helen was directed to expose herself to the body consciousness of others. She did this by mingling with people in local shopping malls and by eating out frequently. By nature, Helen was a very friendly person and mixed easily with all kinds of people. Sometimes, when she was tired in a mall, she sat on a bench while Fred and Ann window-shopped nearby. Helen might sit there for ten or fifteen minutes chatting with another person. In that brief time, complete strangers poured out to her all the details and troubles of their lives. She always listened with quiet intensity while the Christ lifted their pain and burdens. When Fred and Ann rejoined her, it never failed to amaze them just how warmly the other person felt towards Helen after such a short contact. These little shopping excursions also took their toll on Helen with much clearance work needed afterward to understand the energies involved and how they affected her body.

Not all of Helen's public mingling went so well. One of the most potentially contentious situations was dining out. Helen never demanded anything of anyone but she did expect to be treated civilly. She also believed it her right to be free from having anyone unconsciously dump their problems on her. This was the pattern she encountered with many food servers who assumed that this behavior was justified if they were having a bad day or didn't feel appreciated by management or customers.

Apparently, the high level of creative energy flowing through Helen's aura and body intimidated some people more than others. Automatically, the energy seemed to draw to Helen the most unconscious and rebellious elements in a restaurant environment. If there was a problem in management, service or food preparation, the person most likely to express the problem outwardly seemed to be magnetized to Helen. When it became apparent that this was the situation, Fred, Ann (and Jef, who moved to Jackson in late 1983) cringed and silently wanted to leave.

Helen did not like confrontations with others but often her weakened physical condition would give a psychic signal to some individuals that she was a sponge who would take anything they had to dump. A big mistake! Helen was understanding and even compassionate to a point. However, when it was clear that there was more than just the person's psychic energy coming at her, immediately she took action. She always stood up for herself and deftly, with a well placed word or by an unexpected gesture, she could defuse a potentially hostile situation.

Generally speaking, the level and potency of the Christ's transforming energy working in Helen's body seemed to threaten and intimidate some people unconsciously through the matter of their bodies. At first, others might appear uncomfortable or insecure around her. Many times when this happened in public, (especially those situations involving some kind of service capacity), people would inevitably drop or knock things over, become confused, disoriented or even seem downright incompetent. She would comfort them with several kind words in acceptance of their apology. However, at other times the situation would escalate into outright irritation or hostility towards Helen. No doubt the people involved had had their own problems that day, but the reactions always seemed quite disproportionate to the situation. The reason for this was that these individuals' psychic reactions attracted a more potent source of similar energy from the area's collective unconscious.

The collective unconscious is the interconnection and sum total of people's individual unconscious energies that exist on the unseen human realms. It is an entity, very alive and active in every situation between people and the environment at all times. It interacts with the body and nature consciousness to maintain the human status quo. It challenges and battles with the Christ presence in individuals to prevent changes from finding their way into conscious awareness and external behavior. This is especially so in regards to changing biological matter.

The unseen human body consciousness is often the first line of defense against change. In threatening situations, inexplicably it can compel people to behave or act in ways that resist these potential changes. Through these public events, this level of collective earth force consciousness tried to contain and deny Helen and the energy changing her biological body a place to be in the outer world. The collective unconscious used these routine and irritating situations of everyday life most effectively as an opportunity to prove to all present that Helen was prone to irrational behavior.

To those who live their lives completely unconscious of the inner dimensions of human life, Helen's confrontational behavior was an easy target for their judgment and condemnation. Helen, though, did not have the luxury of unconsciousness. She had to live her life completely aware of the negative effects unconscious energies create in human life. Her multidimensional awareness of and sensitiveness to the turbulent, and often dangerous, psychic forces in this unseen realm compelled her to learn how to protect her bodies from being harmed by it.

Generally speaking and in less charged situations, Helen made quite an impression on others at first meeting. Feeling rich in the Spirit of God's Grace, she outwardly expressed opulence in her physical countenance and elegant bearing. This extended to her home where the furnishings and decor also were qualified with beauty and refinement. With this underlying radiance in her physical appearance, often people thought her wealthy enough to lead a life of leisure. This image was accentuated greatly because she and Fred didn't seem to work like everyone else and out of a need for Helen's physical comfort, they drove a large luxury car.

It was easier for them to let people believe what they wanted. What was not apparent to others was that Helen and Fred were living off the proceeds of the sale of the Colorado Springs house. And other than a few gifts from people, they had no other source of income. As usual, they made the move to Jackson on faith not knowing how long the proceeds would last and what God had in mind to support them. By 1984 they ran out of money altogether. To make matters worse that year, they lost Helen's house in Guntersville to foreclosure. From 1984 through 1994, Helen and Fred were supported by Ann. This support was later augmented by Jef after he got settled in Tennessee.

These instances of financial instability made the next several years a very difficult period for Fred. In his role of care and keeping of Helen, he was challenged daily to release his own concerns and limitations in consciousness to receiving God's support. Helen managed to soothe and lift Fred's spirits which helped to give him the confidence to go on. As a result, he was able to resolve his confusion regarding his commitment as well as his role and purpose in supporting Helen in the New Body work. In the middle of various aspects of crisis and pressure, Helen was the one who constantly remained a clear and distinct channel for the Grace of God to flow into their lives.

Although not then living with Helen and Fred, Ann and Jef were their only help and conscious support for the years of difficult energy work ahead. They all felt woefully inadequate and unprepared for the task. There were times when the three of them joked with Helen about what she had done wrong to be surrounded by such incompetents. In response, Helen said that she too was an incompetent when it came to building a New Body. After all, it was God who would get them all through it, and as far as she knew, God never asked anyone to do a job who was not able to do it - whether they knew it or not!

In late March 1983, Helen stood on a wobbly footstool to try to adjust a ceiling heat register. From the other room Fred heard a loud thud and ran in to find Helen on the floor. She could not move her right arm or shoulder and was in excruciating pain. After getting her into bed and somewhat calmed, the Avatar told her she had broken her arm and shoulder. He went on to say that unfortunately this was part of the energy process necessary for Helen's New Body. Perhaps some background information on Helen's perspective of matter and the physical body might help explain.

Behind all form in the natural world are underlying elements of energy life called devas. These devic and elemental beings also are integral in the actual creation of human life. Their energy animates, coalesces and directs the activities and functions of the biological body as a unified whole. The level of consciousness these beings express through the body is what is called body consciousness. (This is not the same as what is commonly known as body awareness. Body awareness comes through human sense perception and establishes the personality's identity with the body.) Beyond this, there is a level of Soul feeling which is higher than the body's sense of feeling. This level of feeling directly connects the Soul through the devic consciousness to the matter of the physical body.

This devic or body consciousness is only aware of its limited function and purpose in keeping the body alive and functioning for the Soul or Embodying Ego. In the process of doing this, the individual and collective devic energy life evolves through the interaction of body consciousness and human consciousness in the natural world. The consciousness and biological changes brought about by this interplay of devic and human kingdoms infused with the energy of the Christ is known as evolution.

A very important aspect of devic life in the human body is the "breath-form." This energy form represents the devic life pattern necessary to create the physical body as we know it. Although its energy mechanisms and structures extend throughout the entire body, its main connection to the body is in the thoracic region, with very strong connections into the heart and lungs. It is the supervising intelligence of the human physical body for the central devic being (called the body elemental) and the other little beings of the physical elements that actually make up the body. Through its light pattern body or energy matrix, the breath-form acts as a bridge between inner spiritual energies and the outer physical body nature. When the breath-form departs at death, the body elemental is unable to sustain bodily life, the individual biological cells lose their unity and cohesive purpose and grow randomly until body disintegration or decomposition occurs.

The Avatar told Helen that the time had come for her existing body breath-form to depart so that the one for the New Body could replace it. However, despite its weakened condition (from the bombardment by the unconscious force in matter from the area), it still had enough residual energy to resist. It could not however, direct and support arm and shoulder healing activities within the body and resist its removal at the same time. Therefore, the falling incident was being used by the Avatar to put the old breath-form into trauma so it could be extracted.

In the meantime, the Holy Spirit poured a kind of fiery liquid energy into Helen's shoulder and arm that solidified as its vibration slowed down to her body rhythm. This hardened energy held her arm and shoulder in place just like a physical cast. The way it looked on the inner was like aerosol liquid foam insulation when it expands and hardens as it dries. The process of extraction of the old breath-form and insertion of the new one took about four months with Helen restricted to bed.

Life with Helen rarely slowed down. In many ways, once physical body changes began to take place in Helen, the bedroom became her office and the bed her desk. Regardless of what was going on or how she felt, her life focus just shifted to wherever she needed to be at the time. Fred and Ann had to learn how to make these immediate and frequent adjustments with Helen. Everything was new and unpredictable. They had to continually adapt in order to flow with an inner life directed by energy as it unfolded through Helen.

During the initial months of the change out of the breath-form, Fred spent most of his time caring for Helen and doing clearance work. Ann's role during this time was to relieve Fred when needed as well as to take care of the many regular household tasks. Finally, in late July 1983, the Avatar told Helen that the New Body breath-form was in place but it would take about eight to ten years for it to gain enough strength to take over sufficiently to control and effectively operate her body functions.

What this meant was that the New Body breath-form was like an infant's breath-form when it is born. As with any infant, the new form needed to gain the same kind of experience as a child would growing into adulthood. It had to develop within her adult body, being conditioned by her life experience and consciousness each step of the way. She was told that once it reached an adult status, the physical matter the New Body needed to recreate Helen's new outer form would be drawn to it automatically. The matter to fill out her New Body had already been prepared on inner planes and was being held in a kind of matter pool, until she was ready to receive it. However, there was still a lot of old body breakdown and energy work to accomplish.

When Jeffery and Brenda's first child was born in early 1984, they had all become close enough for Helen, Fred and Ann to joyfully join with Jeffery in the hospital waiting room. They were delighted to share with him in the birth of his daughter, Nancy. Helen felt an immediate bond that was so strong that from then on she referred to Nancy as her "little love." As Nancy got older and came to stay at their house, she played for hours in the same room with Helen, seemingly happy just to be around her. After Nancy's birth, Jeffery and Brenda grew closer and more comfortable with Helen, Fred, Ann and Jef. A second child, Will, was born in 1986 and this renewal of their relationship continued to improve. Helen felt as close to Will as she did to Nancy. Somehow God had managed to reunite Helen with Jeffery while shielding him and his family from the drastic realities of her life and energy work.

In early October 1983, Helen's father died suddenly. At the time she was in a very tentative and delicate condition with the new breath-form. Because of this she was unable to participate in the family activities surrounding his death. This may have led others to believe she was not devastated or saddened by his death. She was, but she just didn't have enough vital energy to join in as she wanted.

Therefore, she was forced to grieve silently and privately without the love and support other family members received from each other. In her own way, she released her father and her pain to God and moved on with her work.

As it turned out, around late 1985, Helen's new breath-form started drawing on the New Body matter from that inner pool. Although the energy patterns for the new mental, emotional, etheric and physical bodies had been issued some years before, they had not been completely formed in New Body matter. This started a long and tedious process of accumulating, organizing and differentiating it body by body. Starting with the mental body, it was worked down through the emotional body and concentrated in the etheric body before making its move to replace Helen's biological matter in early 1994. When the new matter started coming into Helen's mental body, she found that because it had been prepared on inner planes, it had no relationship to the earth or its recorded history.

To remedy this condition, in early 1986 Helen began the process of drawing energy into this matter by reading and studying "The Lincoln Library of Essential Information" and Will and Ariel Durant's eleven-volume "The Story of Civilization." Mealtimes were especially enlightening for the next few years. Helen used these times to engage and challenge Fred, Ann and Jef to expand their consciousness. She internalized all that she studied about world history and related it to her metaphysical knowledge of energy emanations and the development of human consciousness through the evolutionary process. With that framework in place, she interrelated and synthesized within herself the elements of psychology, philosophy, religion, mythology, politics, science and art with the spiritual perspectives of occult science, metaphysics and cosmology.

These informal daily mealtime discussions developed into actual classes. Helen conducted these classes quarterly during a period of several years. This was done during visits to East Tennessee for energy work on her body. Although immensely challenging and educational for Fred, Ann and Jef, primarily these classes were for Helen. They gave her a structure in which to push herself into higher understanding by creating a need to have deeper insights from which to teach. Helen was a very resourceful person and never missed an opportunity to find a way to keep herself growing and transmuting. She said that since the Avatar was teaching her through the work on her body, she would pass on what she learned as long as she was able. Weakened by the energy work going on within her, often Helen was not strong enough to sit up while giving classes. So, when traveling, she simply gave the classes from her motel room bed.

# Chapter Three

From their marriage in 1977 through late 1986, Helen and Fred moved residences nine times across three states. By now, constant change and movement was their way of life. Regardless of how long they planned to live somewhere and whether it was a rental apartment or their own home, each residence was redecorated and furnished with loving care. This was done consciously to anchor creative energy making each a warm and protected environment for their life and work. After arriving in Jackson, they spent considerable time looking for a home to buy. Although there were few that caught their attention, they did become acquainted with Jackson and the surrounding areas. During several of these house-hunting excursions, they found themselves driving past a particular property in Humboldt. It seemed to be in an area that met all of their needs but it was not for sale. A couple of years later they were delighted when it came on the market and they were able to buy it.

Humboldt is a small, rural town about fifteen miles northwest of Jackson. It had a population of about 7,500 and a small-town atmosphere where everyone knew everyone else, or thought they did. The neighborhood where their house was located was just outside of the town limits and in a woodsy and fairly isolated subdivision. Everything about the area was secluded and that was the way the people living there wanted it. Deliveries, service calls and neighbors' visitors were the only outsiders who usually ventured down this dead-end road.

The property was lovely with almost three acres of land on a heavily wooded lot. One especially nice feature of the house was a huge great room with a vaulted ceiling reaching nearly twenty feet high. On one wall, there were windows that extended from the floor to the ceiling offering a spectacular view of the surrounding area. Although the house was a diamond in the rough, it was perfect for their needs and lifestyle. In late 1986, Helen, Fred, Ann and Jef moved into the house.

This was to be Helen's personal retreat home for the focus of her New Body work. In the process of following her inner direction to establish a retreat, she discovered that traditional beliefs of isolation, far from the distractions of life, did not fit the bill for a modern-day retreat. In today's world it was better to be hidden in plain sight. She believed this was generally necessary for people (as it was for Fred, Ann and Jef) to learn how to create a protected inner environment along with an outer image to be able to be and work in the world, not isolated from it.

145

Fred spent much time and effort remodeling the home and grounds to suit and support the needs of their work. Helen used the process of working out the details of remodeling and redecorating any home as the practical pattern and structure for working on her body. Her home was her creative workshop for energy qualification.

After the initial interior changes were complete, many overgrown trees and shrubs were removed in preparation to begin landscaping with terraced gardens, flowering trees, shrubs and plants. Physically this work was necessary to anchor and beautify the land with Christ energy. From an inner standpoint it was necessary to attract higher devic energy into the grounds and property to support and protect the work going on within. Although the creative process is similar, working to requalify wild nature is somewhat different than working to requalify a house. The materials used to remodel or redecorate a house have already gone through several stages of refinement through human design and processing before they become lumber, fabric, paint or wallpaper. This normal processing requalifies the raw materials into a conditioned form for practical use.

In the natural world, lower nature beings are unconditioned by human consciousness and are wild and resistant to change. Often they psychically attack those who dare to interrupt the natural order of things. Through this work, Fred learned how to face and work with this underlying wild energy and to release and transmute what it instinctively activated in his bodies. This was done by invoking the Christ energy into every detail of the work to recondition the elemental nature forces into serving a higher plan for Christ expression. With this energy structure in place, a new order of spiritual beings was able to take up residence in the house and grounds.

Helen was involved as much as possible in all the various aspects of the project from design to plant selection and placement. Since Fred did most of the physical work himself, this took several years to accomplish. When finished, the house and property were radiant. Helen named the house "Long Shadows." She dearly loved the long shadows cast by the large oak trees at dusk and dawn. To Helen, these were the magical parts of each day. It was a time for meditation, reflection and to praise God for the day just ended or the one ahead. She said that since the reality of a New physical Body is still in the shadows of human consciousness, symbolically the Light from the work of all those working behind the scenes to create it can be glimpsed by reflection during those magnificent daily transitions.

Over the years in the Humboldt house, Helen kept the environment active by changing and rearranging furniture placements as well as rotating everyone through the different bedrooms in the house. Every time she felt personal energy habits begin to harden in the consciousness of Fred, Ann or Jef (or resistance to energy working in her body), she made changes in the house. Sometimes these moves took place rapidly and without warning to put the household into chaos and to disrupt the crystallizing patterns in the matter of the house and everyone's bodies. These surprise moves were necessary to give the Christ energy a window of opportunity to reestablish the needed energy flow.

Many times all that was necessary was to try furniture placements in all possible room configurations before putting it all back the way it was in the first place. It was not the form that was important but the energy of change to accommodate the spiritual energies seeking expression through her life. Always, there was some creative project going on in the house or in the landscape to keep energy moving and change alive in her environment. Helen enjoyed hosting elegant dinner parties, using her finest china, crystal and silver. The various holidays throughout the year were especially active times within the household for celebrations and festivities as an opportunity to draw and express more energy in their lives and in the lives of those who attended.

Helen practiced qualification rituals on herself also. Everything relating to her body she did with great care, concentration, consciousness and with an eye towards beauty. Daily she directed energy into her own body by attentive grooming. She set the tone for each day by how she dressed (even if she never left the house). Bathing and body care were important activities for her. Many times she felt so ill from the energy work that she literally had to discipline herself to keep up her daily schedule. Everything she did was designed to nourish the New Body process and to aid the energy changes taking place within her.

She took every grooming activity deeply into her feelings and body. Her baths were qualified to cleanse away the breakdown and cellular debris of the old and to soothe the growth of the new. Body lotions applied with loving care were part of the ritual which extended protection as the new cells grew out towards the surface of her body. Helen did her hair and make-up not because it was expected of her as a female, but because she truly wanted to give God's work in her body a beautiful face to the world.

She continued with her sewing, making clothes for herself and others. This was qualified as an external expression of the beauty of the spiritual self, while still meeting the need of an outer, practical function. Everything she made was finished exquisitely and tailored to fit the individual's particular style and body type. Often she chose daring color combinations and fabric patterns that by themselves did not seem to go together. However, when finished, the overall effect was stunning. In the process, she also taught Ann and Fred to sew. Many times the work on Helen's body did not allow her to complete every project she began, but under her direction they were finished by either Fred or Ann. All that mattered to Helen was that the energy purpose was accomplished. In fact she always strived to withdraw herself from her many creations to allow them to stand on their own in the energy and purpose for which they were created.

During the late 1980s, the breakdown in Helen's natural body began to show itself physically. She had been going through a cycle for years where her teeth gradually died and fell out. But now she began to lose teeth more regularly. In addition to refusing any medical intervention, Helen had made the decision to refrain from any dental work. This was part of her thoroughness in placing all her needs in God's hands. The loss of teeth was quite visible and prompted her to speak with her hand near her mouth shielding a clear view of it as she spoke.

By 1990, Helen's eyesight was fading rapidly. The Holy Spirit told her that this was all part of the body-building process and that when the new body matter started replacing the old, she would grow new teeth and her eyesight would be restored. The gradual loss of eyesight was more subtle and not readily apparent to Fred and Ann. Helen suspected that it might be too traumatic for them to know about and kept it a secret until it got to the point where all she could see was dim light. All along there were telltale signs, that this was happening which Fred and Ann simply reacted to, rather than interpreting correctly. They thought her sight problems were normal eye deterioration that Helen chose to have God correct rather than an eye doctor. Often they were irritated with Helen over the fact that she had to rely on them, which made their jobs harder.

Finally when they found out just how serious the eye problem was and that it was a major part of the process, their sense of guilt and self-criticism for not being more understanding and supportive almost overwhelmed them. However, Helen knew exactly what was happening and blamed neither for how they reacted to her condition. In time, both Fred and Ann accepted this experience as a sober reminder of Helen's total commitment to the body work and the potential physical consequences if it were not followed through to completion.

Not being able to see people clearly, the television or scenery while out riding in the car were not problems for Helen. To compensate, she developed her hearing sensitivity to the point where in normal situations and activities she heard the sounds and details others did not. Also, she used her inner vision to fill in any picture of what was happening around her. Many times she saw and understood things more clearly in her mind than others did with their external sight.

Helen said the hardest part and real sacrifice for her was not being able to read. She loved to read challenging material and then go into a state of conscious meditation or contemplation while the Holy Spirit taught her what she needed to know from the information. She used this process as a springboard into cosmic realms for new insights and understanding. Although Fred and Ann read to Helen when her sight finally failed, it was not the solitary activity that previously she had so enjoyed.

In early January 1990, Jef moved out of the house.  Three years earlier, he was the one who had initiated buying the Humboldt house for Helen.  With Ann's help, the two of them had managed to purchase the house.  However, before his move, Ann bought out his share of the house so he could concentrate his life near his work in another city.  With just Helen, Fred and Ann living in the house, life changed again.

Although the biological changes taking place in Helen's body were still debilitating, she had actually felt somewhat better and stronger during the past year.  Because of this improvement in her condition, she now encouraged Ann to go back to school to become a certified travel agent.  Helen knew Ann liked to travel and enjoyed making travel arrangements for all their trips.  She also believed this activity might help renew Ann's connection with the outer world.  With Jef gone and Ann driving daily to Memphis for a few months, Helen and Fred had time alone together in the house.  They began to prepare for the day when Helen's New Body was complete and she could once again resume normal worldly activity.

# Chapter Four

In early 1990, Helen began having trouble breathing and experienced problems with her legs. For several months leading up to this time, she could hardly make it up the half flight of stairs from the garage entry. Periodically over the years, Helen had problems like these but they always disappeared with the completion of energy work taking place at the time. Therefore, neither Helen nor Fred attached much significance to her current symptoms. It came as a complete surprise one morning when she told Fred and Ann that the Holy Spirit told her during the night that she was experiencing congestive heart failure. She was assured that her condition was a result of excessive fluid buildup in her body from a recent phase of accelerated decomposition of her natural or old body. Further she said the Holy Spirit promised her that if they followed Its direction, she would survive this present crisis.

This was a critical turning point in Fred's life. Although Helen and he had been through some very difficult physical crises, this was the first time in their life together that he truly feared Helen's life was in peril. In her previous comalike states or periods of physical distress, her old physical body remained strong and vibrant. However, the years of old body breakdown had left her quite fragile and weak. Despite the fact that Fred had been told by Helen that her existing body would eventually be unable to sustain her body life, he chose to believe that somehow this didn't mean the old body would literally die. He convinced himself that the old body death was symbolic rather than actual. Now, the reality of death shook him to the core of his being. He had no control whatsoever over Helen or the energy transformation of her body. At first he was frightened that Helen might die and lose her body if things didn't go as planned. Then, as he prayed for help, God's energy stabilized him so he could get on with supporting Helen's needs and following through with her directions.

To accomplish this, internally Fred reviewed and renewed his pre-marriage agreements with Helen and recommitted himself to honoring the spirit and the form of his promises. No outside medical help was possible. However, Ann was just completing school so once again she was able to assist full time. Jointly they resolved at all costs to do what Helen asked of them and to follow the Holy Spirit instructions, no matter what. With this new development, it was visible and clear that Helen had moved into a life-and-death phase of the body work and to them death was not an option.

One of the major concerns both Helen and Fred had was Jeffery. Helen worried that if he saw her and wanted to know what was going on, he could become terribly frightened and then possibly angered by her refusal to seek medical treatment. If that happened, both Helen and Fred were concerned that he might try to intervene and force her into treatment. Helen asked Fred to do everything possible to keep Jeffery from finding out what was happening to her. This was Fred's next crisis. He was troubled that if something ever happened to Helen, Jeffery might hold him responsible for her death for not getting her the necessary medical attention. But, through prayer and surrender, he found a place within himself to move forward and carry out Helen's wishes. For the next two years, most of Helen's contact with Jeffery and his family was by phone. She saw them only when she was between crises and when she had sufficient vital energy to look somewhat healthy.

During this episode with congestive heart failure, Helen (under the direction of the Avatar and the Holy Spirit) was able to instruct Fred and Ann in her care. At first, the inner medical team, so to speak, kept her anesthetized and asleep while they directed energy into her heart, lungs and body. This was an attempt to complete the inner body work causing the excess physical fluids as soon as possible. Gradually, the fluid buildup made it impossible for her to rest comfortably, even with energy anesthetization. She became physically distressed and agitated. All Fred and Ann could do was make her as comfortable as possible, care for her needs, and do as much clearance work as was necessary. After about three months, Helen started to feel better and the fluid level around her heart and lungs started to decrease. However, the fluid buildup in her lower body and legs remained a problem.

Once Helen felt better, she didn't want to stay in bed. Any reason to get up she embraced with enthusiasm. Every time she wanted to get up to do something for herself, either Fred or Ann jumped to assist her. She felt smothered and told them that what she wanted most was the freedom to at least try to get around on her own. One day while returning from the bathroom, Helen's legs gave way. The fall seriously injured her right knee, leg and hip. This was a terrible setback for her. However, from an energy perspective, the fall began the process of separating the lower part of her old physical body from its energy connection to the earth. The Avatar told her that she would not be able to walk without assistance until this disconnection process was complete and her New Body energy had taken up residence in her lower body. This meant that for the time being, she could no longer get around without Fred's help and a wheelchair.

By spring of 1991, generally Helen was much better and didn't need as much constant care. Feeling better, she encouraged Ann to look for a job, now that she had completed her certification program. Shortly thereafter, Ann did find work as a travel agent and resumed a somewhat normal lifestyle and social life. By that summer, Helen had made friends with her wheelchair and she and Fred had worked out ways of getting her around the house and taking her out for excursions around town. The hardest part was figuring out how Fred could take her into public restrooms without causing pandemonium. Once this was worked out, going out in public was not only possible but enjoyable for Helen.

Helen's condition during the past year had interrupted their semiannual trips to the hot springs in Colorado. However this spring, the Avatar suggested Helen go there so the physical waters could help draw out the excess fluid in her lower body. They went and Helen was able to continue with the trips for about another year. The healing energies working on her body increased her mobility to the point where for short periods of time she was able to get around with a walker. In fact, her spirits were so high after returning from the Colorado trip that, in spring 1992, she felt good enough for Fred, Ann and herself to rotate their bedrooms again. This was necessary in order to clear out the accumulated energy crystallization from the past two years of her convalescence. There wasn't time or energy to organize anything other than Helen's room before the next critical phase of Helen's body work began in early summer.

Helen was once again relatively comfortable traveling by car. In fact she was so heartened by how well she made the spring trip to Colorado that she and Fred bought a new car in preparation for more travel. Still, Helen couldn't get around without a walker or wheelchair, but she felt and looked more like her old self. Both Helen and Fred were relieved and deeply grateful for the guidance they'd been given and were humbled by the power of the Christ to transform Helen's body to date. Her New Body work was on schedule and everything seemed to be going as the Avatar had planned.

In June, for Fred's birthday that year, Helen suggested that they drive to Memphis for the weekend as a little getaway from the confines of the house and the chaos over the recent room changes. But this short trip to Memphis did not go well at all. While they were having breakfast in Memphis, Helen told Fred that she was not feeling well and that the Avatar told her to return home immediately. On the way home, she explained that she was entering a dangerous phase of energy work to push the New Body matter to cross over from her etheric body into her dense physical body.

The pain she experienced during the internal breakdown of her old body had been like a clarion call to the New Body matter pool on inner planes to descend into her bodies. As expected, it responded and descended plane by plane, body by body, until it had filled out the matter of all of her subtler bodies. These were critical steps in the process. Unless the New Body level of matter crossed the divide between its subtle energy state in her etheric double to take dense form in her physical body, her body would not be able to support biological life much longer. By late 1992, after about a year and a half at her job, Ann had to discontinue her outer life to help Fred full time with Helen's care.

Up until this point, all of the work involved internal organ and systems changes. With this current phase, Helen's external appearance began to change drastically. Ever since she started traveling to Los Angeles for the I AM Reading Room activities, Helen gained and carried considerable weight. In many ways this added to her physical energy presence. Despite the weight, she looked good with good muscle tone and magnificent light olive complexion. By early 1993, she had lost considerable weight and her skin coloring had turned pallid. Once again the fluid buildup in her body was causing her severe pain as well as breathing and mobility problems. In physical death, the first step is the breakdown of solids into gases and fluids, and Helen's solid body was dissolving while she was still in it.

Paraphrasing from the "Bardo of Dying" in "The Tibetan Book of the Dead," the four great elements of Helen's body were collapsing one into the other. She felt as if she were being crushed by mountains, tossed by waves, scorched and carried off by a strong wind. The whole point of the Tibetan dying ritual is that prior to death there is a need to reacquaint a person with the true essence of their spiritual nature. This is so they can separate consciously from their body as their worldly identity. This ritual makes liberation from physical life more meaningful and aids in the transition to their new reality in preparation to reembody.

However, Helen did not intend to die along with her old physical body. Although she separated her consciousness from her old body to release it, she could not allow her consciousness to depart the physical plane. It was needed to coalesce and infuse the essence of New Body matter as it replaced the matter of the dying body. This was essential! She had to maintain her consciousness on the physical plane no matter how traumatic the old body death process became.

Helen had been preparing for what was about to happen from the time she consciously committed to face death and break its limitation. This final stage of the process would put everything she had worked for on the line. She had long since passed the point of no return and going forward was her only option to fulfill her purpose and to sustain her life in the world. She had much protection and help from the inner team working with her as well as Christ energies surrounding her.

Helen trusted the preparations made by the Avatar to minimize the reactions in Fred and Ann's bodies but she didn't think she could withstand reactions from Jeffery, his family or hers. Anyone who has witnessed life-threatening illness or trauma, knows that there is a profound psychological and physical reaction to the experience. For the past two years, Fred had closely monitored visits, but in 1993 Helen asked him to block all attempts by anyone to visit their home. He did everything he could to maintain the existing level of relationship with Jeffery and to ease everyone's concern over not being able to see Helen. There was no perfect, easy or right way to accomplish this mission. As a result, Fred felt his relationship with Jeffery deteriorate.

From early 1993 to mid-1994, Helen suffered greatly but maintained her positive spirit and consciously directed her care. Fred and Ann divided up the responsibilities for Helen's care and the daily household duties. Helen needed to remain conscious as to what was going on at all times. Because she could not breathe easily in a reclining position, the Holy Spirit only allowed her brief periods of sleep spread throughout the day and night. This meant that at all times either Fred or Ann had to be awake in Helen's room. A good period of rest for them was two hours of uninterrupted sleep.

Often, Helen would just sit quietly for hours at a time with her eyes wide open in a state of detachment from her body. Both Fred and Ann learned to adapt to this and to listen carefully to the rhythm of her breathing. If it was even and smooth she was okay. However, even the slightest change was an early warning of some problem beginning to surface. Fast action was then necessary to do clearance work in order to direct energy to ease Helen's panic and to help correct the problem until the crisis passed.

Sometime in early spring of 1994, things suddenly began to improve. Helen became more animated, had the energy to speak more and her color began to return. In addition, she again felt able to do clearance on herself with Fred. Refraining from doing clearance was hard on Helen. Since everything in her life started on the inner and moved into her outer life, the information it revealed was essential. To again be able to personally identify what was happening on these inner realms was a thrill and comforted her.

During one of the clearance sessions, it was revealed that the inflow of New Body matter from her etheric double to her physical body had started and was picking up speed. Daily, Helen delighted in the positive changes she could feel taking place. One day she asked Fred to look at what she thought was a broken tooth fragment sticking out of her gum. As Fred probed and studied it, he realized that it was not a tooth fragment but rather a new tooth just breaking through her gum line. Helen was ecstatic! This was the first physical sign and evidence that the matter pool transfer from her etheric double to the physical had taken place and that her New Body was beginning to grow.

By early summer of that year, things had changed drastically but not in the direction they had hoped. It happened so gradually that neither Fred nor Ann noticed it at first. By the time they recognized what was happening, the consciousness that Fred and Ann knew as Helen seemed to have departed. This meant Helen was no longer able to consciously direct her care or participate in the process going on in her body. It was at this point that they began taking care of Helen's bodily needs and had to begin dealing with her body elemental.

As mentioned earlier, the body elemental is the central devic being in the body. It manages the day-to-day activities of the elemental life operating and animating the biological body. When the consciousness of the person living in the body is anchored and functional, the body elemental is passive and maintains the body unconsciously through the involuntary systems. When the embodying ego withdraws its consciousness connection to the body, the body elemental is the only major consciousness living in the body. It then takes on the active role of controlling the voluntary systems and replaces the person as the personality in the body. Because its realm is unconsciousness, usually it expresses outwardly what was projected into the body by the person's subconscious, the personal unconscious and the collective unconscious. This is a typical situation in nursing homes where the spiritual essence of the individual has left and the body elemental is controlling the last vestiges of life in the body.

Slowly, the fluid accumulation in Helen's body worsened causing open sores on her legs in order to release fluids. Several times a day Fred bathed and disinfected her legs to ease the effects and pain of this condition. She could no longer move around without Fred's help and only then with great pain and difficulty. By early fall, she was barely able to assist Fred at all in his care for her. She was in severe pain at all times and even the slightest movement of her skin over the bed sheets caused unbearable pain. This led to tears and the berating of Fred or Ann over their treatment of her.

With each day, conditions worsened. One day in late September everything came to a crisis point. The fluid buildup in Helen's body not only made her life and breathing unbearable, but the lack of oxygen to her brain was forcing her consciousness further away from the physical plane. It seemed an impossible situation. After a round of severe difficulties at midday, Helen suddenly shocked both Fred and Ann by declaring that she did not want Fred to care for her any longer. She demanded he phone Jeffery to come and take over. No amount of discussion could dissuade her from this action. Physically and psychologically drained, Fred phoned him.

Jeffery had not seen his mother in a very long time. When he walked into her room the shock in his eyes and face was overwhelming. Helen's body elemental started right in on him and told Jeffery she wanted him to take care of her and that she no longer wanted Fred around. In that moment and thereafter, there was no way for Fred to explain adequately to Jeffery that the person he knew as his mother was no longer able to speak with him, and that when the pain got too much for Helen, she withdrew leaving the irrational body elemental to react in severe pain.

In a shattered condition himself and without mentioning the New Body work, Fred tried to explain to Jeffery that Helen wanted God to heal her. Amazingly, Jeffery was calm and rapidly recovered his composure while he took in everything as best as he could. When he spoke, Jeffery told Helen that he could not take care of her in the same way as Fred. But if he agreed to help, she would have to go to the hospital for treatment. At this point Helen was connected enough with her body to refuse. However, after a long period of negotiating with Jeffery, the pain of being in the body got so bad that again she withdrew and the body elemental agreed to his conditions just to get some relief.

Within an hour she was in the hospital emergency room now raising a ruckus over being there. Again, Helen touched down into her body only to find things had been taken out of her control and that she was in the hospital. Fred was well acquainted with this constant shift from Helen to her body elemental but how to explain it reasonably to Jeffery or anyone else was beyond his capacity at the time. Left ungoverned by the human Spirit, a body elemental is a formidable force to deal with when it assumes someone's body identity. Eventually, Helen's had run Fred into exhaustion.

As Fred sat in the emergency room listening to Helen, he was filled with a sense of failure in fulfilling his trust with God as well as failing Helen. He prayed constantly trying to release his guilt. What he feared most was happening. Helen was in the hospital and he was frightened she would not leave alive. This is what she had told him in the beginning and he believed her. But because he was so physically and psychologically spent, there was nothing he could do to change the course of events as they were being played out. As always, it was in God's hands, but for Fred this seemed more true than ever before. As he released the load of his burdens to God, Fred felt relief and a warm loving energy enter and surround him.

# Chapter Five

Helen was diagnosed with severe pneumonia as well as bilateral lymph edema and severe stasis dermatitis and cellulitis in her lower extremities. Simply stated, this meant that without immediate treatment, she would certainly develop gangrene in her legs and if that didn't kill her, congestive heart failure would. Her condition was a direct result of the fluid pressure causing constrictions on her heart and circulatory system from the breakdown of her old body. From Helen's New Body perspective, this was a positive development but from a medical viewpoint, it was as bad as it could get.

As it turned out, her hospital stay was a disaster. Helen struggled to maintain her conscious connection to restrain and direct her body elemental. At that point, it was fighting to keep her body from dying. This created an internal battle between her consciousness and body elemental for control. Helen consistently refused all medical treatment other than her daily whirlpool leg baths to restore healthy skin tissue to her legs. She was desperate and felt captive by her "medical condition" as well as by those who wanted her in the hospital. To stay true to her purpose, resistance to treatment and medical authority was her only option. She spit out all medication given her and regularly pulled out her catheter. When Jeffery found out she would not take treatment or cooperate with her doctor, he withdrew from her care and stopped coming to see her. Who could blame him. His mother was dying before his eyes and she wouldn't let him do anything to help save her.

With Jeffery now out of the picture, Fred found himself caught in a precarious position. He explained to the doctors and medical staff, countless times, that Helen wished only to be healed directly by God and would not accept their help. He further explained that this was nothing new and had been her life-long position. The more difficult point to explain was why she was in the hospital in the first place. But no reasonable explanation was possible. Time and again, well-meaning people explained to Fred that God also worked through doctors and medicine. They believed that Helen was delusional in her stance that God could heal her directly without their help.

Everyone wanted Fred to find some way to force Helen to take treatment. After all, if she survived, she would surely thank him for intervening. In his heart, he knew the truth. If somehow he found a way to intervene and medicine saved her life, she would never forgive him for not giving her the freedom to live or die based on her own relationship with God.

The attempts to force Helen to take treatment grew so intense that Helen's assigned doctor had her examined by a state mental health professional who proclaimed her competent to refuse treatment. After ten days, this was the last straw for her doctor. He immediately discharged Helen because there was nothing more he could do for her. After Jeffery's withdrawal and her discharge from the hospital, Helen once again accepted Fred and Ann's care.

There were several very positive outcomes from Helen's hospital experience. The first was that by hiring sitters to stay with Helen at night while she was in the hospital, both Fred and Ann had ten days of badly needed rest. Next, Helen established a very loving relationship with one of the nursing assistants, who agreed to continue on with Helen at home. Helen's agreement to have in-home help, made it possible for Fred and Ann to hire other nursing assistants to sit with her at other times of the day and night. In the hospital, Fred and Ann also learned how to better treat Helen's leg condition in their home using a portable whirlpool.

Most importantly, Helen did not die in the hospital and returned home, more determined than ever to see the New Body work through to its end. Apparently her fight to resist any forced treatment rallied her departing consciousness to assist her in her need of increased spiritual Will.

With the assistance of home care, life was remarkably better for everyone. Within a few weeks, two very loving and competent nursing assistants (who were sisters) were hired to complete a daily shift. Helen now had new people to get to know and to talk to. But she was definitely not talking about or speaking from anything close to physical plane reality. As the fluid pressure increased in her body, the brain damage caused by oxygen deprivation began to weaken Helen's connection to the body. Again, her consciousness departed, and she started living her life on an inner plane just above her physical body. But, she had enough connection to her brain to use her voice to speak about what she was experiencing in her inner world, although often what she spoke made no sense to those around her.

This did not seem to matter to the aides. Often, as Fred relieved either of them in the early mornings, he found them singing hymns with Helen. Helen could not carry a tune, but that did not matter. The love of God coming through her voice more than made up for singing off key. In a strange and magical way, her transcendent love of God lifted her voice into a kind of ethereal harmony with those singing along with her. It was quite a scene to behold.

One day in late November 1994, Helen announced to Fred and Ann that the Christ told her to go to the hospital. This was not her body elemental speaking, it was Helen and she was clear and adamant. Once satisfied that it was Helen speaking, both Fred and Ann were elated. For so long there seemed to be no support or help for them in the outside world. Perhaps somehow the Christ was going to use medicine to complete her New Body and, because of this, Helen would agree to treatment.

But as soon as Helen was settled into an emergency examination room, she started to yell at Fred and Ann for bringing her into the hospital again. She couldn't remember that the Christ had told her to come in the first place. Surprisingly though, Helen was silent during the examination and got along fairly well with the emergency room doctor. Afterward she seemed pleased that he was admitting her. During the wait for her room, she became agitated and once again started screaming at Fred and Ann. They tried to calm her so she would lower her voice, but all that did was incite her even more. Then, with almost frightening clarity of voice and consciousness in her eyes, she said, "Fred, just what will it take for you to be willing to break the human laws of matter to serve God?" This hit Fred like a bolt of lightning! It was as if a tone from God gave Fred a blow in his consciousness and began to clear the confusion out of his mind and bodies. It was now clear to him that the Christ had orchestrated this hospital visit for him, not Helen. The trauma of this experience and breakthrough brought him closer to Helen's purpose than ever before.

Later that night, as Helen was getting settled into her room she suddenly asked Fred to take her home. Just to be sure, Fred reminded her that it was the Christ who told her to come to the hospital. Helen's response was clear and direct, "Fred," she said, "that is entirely true, but He did not say I should take treatment." This brief exchange made it clear between them that whatever happened from this point on was up to the Christ, not them. This was further emphasized when the admitting doctor required Helen and Fred to sign a waiver stating that Helen was leaving the hospital against the strong treatment recommendations of her doctor. They were certain she was going to die.

By early January 1995, Helen's condition had worsened considerably. She had broken a leg in a fall and could no longer get out of bed for any reason. The effect of this on her old body was immediate and devastating. Again, Helen's consciousness began departing and her body elemental took over, forcing Fred and Ann to deal with it rather than the Helen they knew and loved. However, there was a major difference this time. This was because the broken leg also broke the spirit of Helen's body elemental, and greatly decreased its ability to hold its place in her body. Its replacement with a new body elemental was crucial to completing the New Body. Without this higher level of body elemental in place, her physical body would die.

From his revelations in the hospital, Fred had entered into a new trust with God which gave him a new meaning and partnership role in Helen's life and New Body work. Out of necessity, he had learned how to speak telepathically with Helen's consciousness, now withdrawn from her physical presence and living on inner planes. This level of communication was essential to continue caring for her needs. Since "Helen" was no longer there to give instructions on her care, Fred had also learned how to speak directly with the Avatar for help and guidance. It was as if Fred's conscious connection to Helen's higher consciousness, along with that of the Avatars, acted as a physical bridge to Helen's body. Fred's new relationship with Helen and the Avatar made it necessary for him to stay close to Helen at all times. It seemed to calm her body and make others' care of her possible without hassle.

On Helen's birthday, January 5, Fred took a few hours off to find her a present. Upon returning home, from the other end of the house he heard Helen yelling over and over again at the top of her lungs "Venus, Virgo, Mercury, Mars!" As he entered her room, Ann told him that over an hour ago, Helen started out softly speaking those words. Gradually she became louder and more agitated. Ann had tried everything to calm her but nothing had worked. At first it seemed as though Fred's telepathic connection to Helen and the Avatar had vanished because he could not get either of them to speak to him. As he calmed his frayed nerves with prayer for guidance, he suddenly understood what was happening.

Helen was using this simple astrological mantra to connect and anchor her consciousness in her body's physical brain in order to speak with him. Immediately, as he voiced this outwardly to her, her agitation dissipated. She continued to speak the same words over and over for another twenty minutes or so, but now in a rather calm, clear and determined way. Then in a soft, tentative but distinct voice of the person Fred knew as Helen spoke and said:

"Fred, I am tired and I am going to die. Would you please let me go so I can leave?" For Fred it was as if his heart had been ripped from his chest. Even in the deepest sanctuary of his heart and mind, he never believed this day would ever come. Helen's real consciousness and voice was the only thing in this world that would convince Fred that it was true. This was why the Avatar had drawn back from him to allow Helen to speak these potent words to him personally. In that moment of total devastation, he was forced to face that this was the final test of his unconditional agreement and willingness to give Helen freedom. It did not matter that his love for her was used by God to intertwine their lives. Or that it was this love connection that kept Helen connected to her body in order to complete the New Body process. His love was now holding Helen to a body that could no longer serve her spiritual purpose or maintain her life. No matter how much Fred wanted and needed Helen to live, he had to release her and complete his trust and agreement by truly setting her free.

With this single event, their Soul union of the spiritual feminine and masculine broke inside Fred. He knew in that instant that God had released him from the last vestiges of his trust for Helen's care and keeping. Within himself, during the next month, Fred did everything he could to release Helen. He withdrew more each day from her and his activities of caring for her. Painfully, he busied himself by planning for a life without Helen. As hard as it was to consider, he prepared himself to leave the house for a trip to Colorado. This was necessary to completely disconnect any residual psychic energy of his or energy structures within him that might even remotely try to hold her in her dying body.

One day, Ann came out of Helen's room and said that she was having trouble breathing and asked to be taken to the hospital. By this time, Fred had detached himself from Helen's behavior enough to know that it wasn't Helen asking but rather her body elemental. Ann knew this also. Fred turned to the Holy Spirit for guidance. As a result, he felt compelled to phone for an ambulance to let the next hospital scene play itself out as it would. Once the emergency medical technician put her on oxygen, the panic in her body elemental subsided and Helen did not want to go to the hospital. Even in the confusion of the moment, Fred stayed with his guidance to go ahead to the hospital.

After x-rays and an emergency room examination, the doctor took Fred aside to tell him that Helen was dying. He said that unless he did something immediately she would not survive a week. Very calmly and without a moment's hesitation, Fred explained that Helen did not want treatment and thanked him for all that he had done. The doctor, stunned, took Fred by the arm and led him into Helen's cubicle. At that point he very lovingly and patiently explained the situation to Helen and told her that Fred had refused all treatment for her and asked her if that was her wish also. After confirming it was, for the first time in months she smiled at Fred and said: "You are now with me all the way. I can't begin to tell you how much this means to me. Thank you!"

After returning home from the hospital, Fred continued with his Colorado travel plans. Helen was definitely calmer. He knew that her death was imminent, but understanding how and why would just have to wait. One day while Fred was helping the home aide change Helen's bed pad, she started gasping for air. After the nurse failed to calm Helen, she turned to Fred for what to do next. Since he had never seen anyone die before, he didn't know she was dying. He just took her in his arms and gently calmed her body elemental until it was breathing calmly and evenly again.

As her breathing was restored and she settled back in bed, she pushed Fred away and glared at him in a way that shocked him to attention. Even though startled, he then realized that he had called Helen back into her body against her will and she was just plain mad at him. The experience of willing Helen back into her body clearly defined for him what he had to do to let her go. Even if it came out of love, it was not his will that was important but rather Helen's. For both Fred and Ann, this near-death event finally let in the realization that Helen was dying. That next week turned to pure hell again as Helen made sure that neither of them would repeat interfering with her death. Every time either of them were in her room, she lashed out at them verbally. All Fred and Ann could do was to surrender to God and allow the Christ to cut each of them loose from Helen so she could depart.

All that week Fred and Ann prepared for Helen's death and tried to help each other release her. On the day before Fred was due to leave for Colorado, he was up early with Helen that morning. Ann relieved him briefly, so he could take a shower. As he returned to the room, Ann met him at the door and said softly, "Fred, I believe Helen just died." Fred walked over to Helen's bed, checked her pulse and gently kissed her good-bye. He then collapsed in a chair for a good cry before phoning Jeffery with the news. The day was February 19, 1995.

# EPILOGUE

On the third day after her death, Helen's body was cremated. At Jeffery's request, there was an informal memorial service at Helen's mother's house in Medina for her mother, the rest of the family and friends. Several days later, in a ritual with myself, Ann, Jef and two others, Helen's ashes were scattered on a mountainside near Glenwood Springs, Colorado. It was an appropriate closure for a magnificent life and a good death.

For six years, I've been engaged in a variety of activities to more fully understand and integrate what I have lived and learned in my life with Helen. Guided by God, writing this memoir has been the point around which my internal search, transmutation and energy work has revolved. Its completion brings to a close an inner phase of recording and transferring the records of Helen's New Body work into a universal, creative pattern in the Christ for myself and others to draw upon.

Why was Helen unable to complete the New physical Body in this embodiment? At present, I cannot say for certain. But I do know that in dying, Helen did not fail in the work or in her commission from God. Her death was a significant advance in the work. It was the final physical act necessary to complete an energy bridge for the Light Pattern of the New Body to cross from the inner, subtle, human etheric body to the outer, dense physical body. She paid the price for this bridge in a life of pain, suffering and isolation. Drastic as her life was, she never saw it as a sacrifice nor did she complain. As difficult as the last five years of her life were for Ann and me, her willing and joyful surrender to the energy and to death somehow made our role in the process possible and bearable.

Helen told me that, in retrospect, I would consider those last years with her the greatest learning experience of my life. I can honestly say she was right. What I've learned and experienced in energy continues to teach me today. However, to get to this perspective, I've had to face and resolve my own doubts and fears about our life. This was not easy because I as reentered the world after her death, I was surrounded by inner and outer pressure to consider her life a failure, to believe that I was duped by Helen and that building a New Body is impossible. This conscious and unconscious pressure tried to convince me that to be accepted by the world, I had to stop communicating about the work and abandon my commitment to carry it forward. There have been times when I thought I had lost the battle. But somehow, the Holy Spirit got me through the darkest periods to help me understand that although Helen is gone, the New Body process is alive in all those committed to carry on the work.

All along Helen said that others who followed her would not go through the same severity in the process as she did. As I proceed with the work, so far I can say that she was correct. But there is pain and mutation involved in any radical, physical change in the body. Having experienced the work with Helen, I know what to expect and how to respond during certain critical phases of the work. This enables me to more consciously cooperate with the inner forces working on my body. Unfortunately, Helen did not have the luxury of knowing beforehand.

Helen was a spiritual pioneer and warrior. Her mission was to give freedom to the Spirit of the Christ to transform the matter of her physical body into a higher human life-form. In the process, the Christ used the work on her body to build an etheric bridge to the physical plane over which higher levels of transforming energy and consciousness can flow to humanity and the planet. Her foe was the evolutionary force in matter that uses unconscious limitations in human and body consciousness to keep the human Spirit bound to the wheel of reembodiment and captured in crystalline matter. She consecrated her life in the service of God and lived life with integrity and courage to the very end.

This was not Helen's first New Body building embodiment and it probably will not be her last. In some embodiment, she or someone else will succeed in the Christ and a New human Body will be a reality for all to see. When that happens, present human limitations in consciousness will be shattered making it possible for energy, matter and the laws of nature to be viewed from a whole new perspective and dimension.

Frederick R. Kipp

# ACKNOWLEDGMENTS

Karen Kipp, my partner and wife, made this memoir possible. Her love, nurturing and encouragement sustained me while I struggled to make sense of my experiences and write what turned out to be a voluminous and unorganized first draft. She took on the very difficult task of organizing it, cutting it down to size and rewriting parts of it to make it readable. This was no small achievement since initially I vigorously resisted her suggested changes. She courageously persevered in guiding me through structural changes and many rewrites before I was able to fully recognize the incredible value of her insightful ability to identify the essential from the nonessential in telling the story and to organize the sequence of events to maintain the flow for the reader. Thank you, Karen, for suffering through the ordeal with me.

Others contributed enormously. Many thanks: To Ann and David Wray for your considerable love, holding and support (both inner and outer) throughout the long writing process. And, Ann for generously and tirelessly sharing in Helen's care for so many years as well as conversing with me about those years in the time since her death.

To Martha and Trevor Mordecai for your encouragement and support of me in writing this book. And, Martha for sharing with me your early experiences with Helen and for being receptive to my writing to you about the things I was trying to work out inside myself.

To Sylvia Anthony, Jane McPherson and Peggy Shanahan for sharing your recollections and memories about the early days of the Children of the Light and I AM Reading Room groups.

To Alison Glascock for your very thoughtful and thorough proofreading and overall review of the manuscript. Your contribution and positive response to the manuscript encouraged me to believe that others who knew Helen might be interested in the book and your suggestions greatly improved the clarity and readability of the story. (Please note that any writing errors that might appear in the book are a result of my revisions after Alison returned the manuscript.)

And finally with deep gratitude to God, thank you Helen for the magnificent Spirit of the Christ your presence on Earth brought to my life and the lives of those who knew you. Thank you for your enormous gift of the New Body pattern to humanity and the world.

F.R.K.

*Frederick R. Kipp*

# SUGGESTED READING

Wambach, Helen, *Life Before Life*, New York, NY, Bantam Books, 1979.
This book is good for people new to exploring and thinking about reincarnation. It contains actual case histories from a psychologist exploring, under hypnosis, life before birth.

Harding, M. Esther, *The 'I' and the 'Not-I'*, A Study in the Development of Consciousness, Princeton, NJ, Princeton University Press, 1973.
This is a good introductory book exploring the basic ideas of Carl Jung's psychology. The writing is direct and in everyday language.

Hamaker-Zondag, Karen, *Astro-Psychology*, New York, NY, Samuel Weiser, Inc., 1980.
A good synthesis of Jungian psychology and astrology showing how, with Jung's principles of synchronicity, the zodiacal signs and planets influence the basic dispositions and psychic makeup of the individual.

Alder, Vera Stanley, *The Initiation of the World*, York Beach, ME, Samuel Weiser, Inc., 2000.
A very direct and eloquent summary of the secret wisdom of the Divine Plan connecting all forms of inner and outer life as one. Alder has a unique talent for condensing and synthesizing the details of esoteric knowledge and its relationship to present day scientific knowledge.

Saraydarian, H., *Cosmos In Man*, Agoura, CA, The Aquarian Educational Group, 1973.
This book proclaims and illustrates that each one of us is a cosmic being in evolution. A very thorough introduction to the esoteric teachings in plain and simple language. He offers detailed definitions and explanations of the many dimensions and subjects presented in metaphysics and occult science.

Heindel, Max, *The Rosicrucian Cosmos-Conception*, Oceanside, CA, The Rosicrucian Fellowship, 1973.
A book discussing Mystic Christianity in relation to occult literature on man's past evolution, present constitution and future development. A good bridge to advanced level reading.

Steiner, Rudolf, *The Gospel of St. John*, Spring Valley, NY, The Anthroposophic Press, Inc., 1984.

This book does a good job of covering initiations in Christianity. Steiner is the founder of Anthroposophy. Although he only authored several books, he lectured extensively in the early part of the twentieth century. These lectures are the source of much of the written material in print under his name today. In addition, he established universities and schools for children to help them make early contact with their Soul and to learn how to synchronize the physical body with the etheric double.

Bailey, Alice A., *Initiations Human and Solar*, 1951, *The Externalisation of the Hierarchy*, 1972, and *Cosmic Fire*, 1973, (or any of her other twenty or so volumes of work) New York, NY, Lucas Publishing Company.

The first two referenced books require an intermediate understanding of metaphysical principles and the last should be considered advanced reading. Bailey discusses The Doctrine of Avatars from pages 285-313 and specifically addresses the Avatar of Synthesis starting on page 301 (5. Divine Embodiments) through the top of page 309 in *The Externalisation of the Hierarchy*.

Percival, Harold Waldwin, *Thinking and Destiny, Being the Science of Man*, New York, NY, The Word Foundation, 1974.

This is definitely advanced level reading for serious initiates, but it very accurately covers some of the challenges a person faces on the Path of Initiation. Based on Helen's work, Percival also accurately describes the preparation needed to build a New Body as well as some of the initial phases.

Blavatsky, H. P., *The Secret Doctrine: The Synthesis of Science, Religion, and Philosophy*, Pasadena, CA, Theosophical University Press, 1974.

This book is the most advanced of its kind in print. Since it was originally published in 1888, the essence energies expressed by Blavatsky within it have continually confounded minds and defied human understanding. It is written spanning so many different inner dimensions that it contains messages for individuals at many different levels of consciousness. Over the past century, many books have been written to try to explain the contents in simple language, but to my knowledge none have succeeded.

**Contact Information:**

For Theosophical Books:
The Theosophical Publishing House
306 West Geneva Road
Wheaton, IL 60187

For Rudolf Steiner Books:
The Anthroposophical Press
R.R. 4, Box 94A1
Hudson, NY 12534

For Alice Bailey Books:
Lucis Publishing Company
113 University Place, 11th Floor
New York, NY 10003

For Harold W. Percival Books:
The Word Foundation
P. O. Box 180340
Dallas, TX 75218

*Frederick R. Kipp*

# ABOUT THE AUTHOR

Frederick R. Kipp was first introduced to the reality of inner life as a young child by his mother. Innately he saw and felt this realm of Energy along with it's Light Rays, Beings and Ascended Masters. This was the beginning of his relationship with his own internal God Presence and the spiritual energies underlying the physical world.

At age thirty he met Helen, a remarkable woman who would become his spiritual teacher. Later he served and supported her work as her student, partner and husband for seventeen years. Since her death in 1995, Fred has continued his spiritual path and commitment to embody and make practical the creative principles of personality and physical transmutation. Writing from his life experiences in spiritual energy and physical transformation work, "A Good Death" is the first of three books in a series entitled "The Avatar Chronicles."

Printed in the United States
2353

9 780759 658011